MW00585775

Moments with Martin Luther

FROM THE LIBRARY OF
Fair Haven
READ IT · LOVE IT · RETURN IT

Also by Donald K. McKim

The Church: Its Early Life
The Authority and Interpretation of the Bible: An Historical Approach
    (with Jack B. Rogers)
The Authoritative Word: Essays on the Nature of Scripture (editor)
Readings in Calvin's Theology (editor)
What Christians Believe about the Bible
A Guide to Contemporary Hermeneutics: Major Trends in Biblical
    Interpretation (editor)
How Karl Barth Changed My Mind (editor)
Ramism in William Perkins' Theology
Theological Turning Points: Major Issues in Christian Thought
Major Themes in the Reformed Tradition (editor)
Encyclopedia of the Reformed Faith (editor)
Kerygma: The Bible and Theology (4 volumes)
The Bible in Theology and Preaching
Westminster Dictionary of Theological Terms
God Never Forgets: Faith, Hope, and Alzheimer's Disease (editor)
Historical Handbook of Major Biblical Interpreters (editor)
Historical Dictionary of Reformed Churches (with Robert Benedetto
    and Darrell L. Guder)
Calvin's Institutes: Abridged Edition (editor)
Introducing the Reformed Faith: Biblical Revelation, Christian Tradition,
    Contemporary Significance
The Westminster Handbook to Reformed Theology (editor)
The Cambridge Companion to Martin Luther (editor)
Presbyterian Beliefs: A Brief Introduction
Presbyterian Questions, Presbyterian Answers
The Cambridge Companion to John Calvin (editor)
Calvin and the Bible (editor)
Historical Dictionary of Reformed Churches, 2nd ed. (with Robert
    Benedetto)
Dictionary of Major Biblical Interpreters (editor)
Ever a Vision: A Brief History of Pittsburgh Theological Seminary, 1959–2009
More Presbyterian Questions, More Presbyterian Answers
A "Down and Dirty" Guide to Theology
Living into Lent
Coffee with Calvin: Daily Devotions
The Westminster Dictionary of Theological Terms, rev. and exp.
Presbyterian Faith That Lives Today
John Calvin: A Companion to His Life and Theology

DONALD K. McKIM

Moments with Martin Luther

95 Daily Devotions

WJK WESTMINSTER
JOHN KNOX PRESS
LOUISVILLE · KENTUCKY

© 2016 Donald K. McKim

First edition
Published by Westminster John Knox Press
Louisville, Kentucky

16 17 18 19 20 21 22 23 24 25—10 9 8 7 6 5 4 3 2 1

All rights reserved. No part of this book may be reproduced or transmitted in any form or by any means, electronic or mechanical, including photocopying, recording, or by any information storage or retrieval system, without permission in writing from the publisher. For information, address Westminster John Knox Press, 100 Witherspoon Street, Louisville, Kentucky 40202-1396. Or contact us online at www.wjkbooks.com.

Scripture quotations from the New Revised Standard Version of the Bible are copyright © 1989 by the Division of Christian Education of the National Council of the Churches of Christ in the U.S.A. and are used by permission.

See Permissions, pp. 101–2, for additional permission information.

Book design by Drew Stevens
Cover design by Allison Taylor

Library of Congress Cataloging-in-Publication Data

Names: McKim, Donald K., author.
Title: Moments with Martin Luther : 95 daily devotions / Donald K. McKim.
Description: First edition. | Louisville, KY : Westminster John Knox Press, 2016. | Includes bibliographical references.
Identifiers: LCCN 2016012181 (print) | LCCN 2016015675 (ebook) | ISBN 9780664261597 (alk. paper) | ISBN 9781611646740 (ebk.)
Subjects: LCSH: Luther, Martin, 1483-1546. | Christian life--Meditations. | Theology, Doctrinal--Meditations.
Classification: LCC BR333.3 .M37 2016 (print) | LCC BR333.3 (ebook) | DDC 230/.41--dc23
LC record available at https://lccn.loc.gov/2016012181

♾ The paper used in this publication meets the minimum requirements of the American National Standard for Information Sciences—Permanence of Paper for Printed Library Materials, ANSI Z39.48-1992.

John Michael Krech

Pastor, theologian, and fellow baseball fan
With appreciation

CONTENTS

PREFACE

I am pleased to offer this Luther devotional book as a comple-
ment to my *Coffee with Calvin: Daily Devotions*.

Martin Luther (1483–1546) is a major character in the
Western world. His influence since the sixteenth century has
been far-ranging, especially in Europe and North America.
Luther has been a fascinating figure, not only for his theological
insights but also for the ways his thought has been used in relation to political, social, and cultural views and practices. But it
is as a theologian, who had a key role in beginning what became
known as the sixteenth-century Protestant Reformation, that
his work has been most enduring. So it is a special pleasure to
present these moments with Luther during 2017, the five hundredth anniversary year of Luther's Ninety-five Theses, when
Luther is remembered and focused on throughout the world.

This is a book of devotional meditations based on short selections of Luther's writings. Nearly all the quotations are drawn
from the American edition of *Luther's Works* (volumes 1–30:
edited by Jaroslav Pelikan [St. Louis: Concordia, 1955–76]; volumes 31–55: edited by Helmut Lehmann [Philadelphia/Minne-
apolis: Muhlenberg/Fortress, 1957–86]; volumes 56–82: edited
by Christopher Boyd Brown (St. Louis: Concordia: 2009–];
cited hereafter as *LW*), the most easily accessible resource for
a vast extent of Luther's writings. New volumes continue to be
translated and made available.

The selections from *LW* are the focus of each devotion. When
quotes are given without a Luther reference, they are from the

selection at the top of the page. Other quotes are cited with reference to the *LW* volume and page number. There are many Luther quotes in the devotions since I've tried to let Luther speak for himself as much as possible.

My goal has been to draw insights from Luther that can be meaningful expressions of Christian faith and action for contemporary Christians. Luther's theological themes have endured for centuries and continue to nourish the faith of millions of Christians today. Christians look to Luther for theological perceptions as well as paths for Christian living. My hope is that these moments with Luther will introduce Luther's wisdom to those who seek theological understanding as well as visions for what God wants disciples of Jesus Christ to be and do by the power of the Holy Spirit.

The book does not, of course, convey the fullness of Luther's thought. This is a task for scholars who draw on Luther's voluminous writings and try to provide an overall coherence and understanding of Luther's important insights. This book cannot explore all aspects of Luther's theological beliefs or his prescriptions for Christian life, since Luther's views on Christian living emerge into many directions.

The book is divided into two major sections: "Believing as a Christian" and "Living as a Christian." This is to indicate, most broadly, that learning from Luther includes what he taught on some of the major aspects of Christian doctrine or Christian belief coupled with his concerns that Christian belief be expressed in the practical aspects of life together in the Christian community, the church, and the life of the Christian in the world.

The book is composed of ninety-five meditations—one, of course, for each of Luther's Ninety-five Theses. Its main structure is sets of seven devotions for thirteen weeks—to encourage a "daily devotion" approach. Each week has an overall theme with devotions devoted to a particular topic of Luther's work. The remaining four devotions have the title "Present and Future." The devotions can be read in any number of ways, and my hope is that they will provide spiritual nourishment whichever method is adopted.

This may be a first acquaintance with Luther for some readers. In days when it is not likely that persons will eagerly turn to major theological tomes, my hope is to provide "bite-sized" bits of Luther. I try to say what Luther means and what implications may be for twenty-first-century persons. As simply and accessibly as possible, I introduce Luther's perceptions and provide a resource that can open some theological as well as devotional or spiritual insights.

Martin Luther was a Christian preacher and teacher. He advocated the approach of the early church theologian Augustine (354–430): that Christian existence is "faith seeking understanding." We study and reflect on Christian faith to gain understanding—of who God is, what God has done, and what God wants us to do. The study of Luther's work can enhance our faith and understanding, during this five hundredth anniversary year . . . and beyond.

Luther wrote, "We should thank God and be happy that our Lord God has shown us the reason for studying, namely, to please Him and to be useful to the world and to improve it. If God grants you something beyond this, then accept it and thank Him for it" (*LW* 68:153). May God grant our studies in Luther will be pleasing to God, useful to the world, and lead to our service to Jesus Christ for the good of the world and its people. Beyond this—for all benefits—we give God thanks and praise!

Donald K. McKim

Germantown, Tennessee
Reformation Day
October 31, 2015

ACKNOWLEDGMENTS

My earliest memory of Martin Luther was watching the 1953 motion picture on Martin Luther, which featured a commentary by the late, eminent Luther scholar Roland H. Bainton of Yale University. Several years after its release, this black-and-white film was often shown in churches. I vividly remember seeing it when I was a child in my home church, the Wampum Presbyterian Church in Wampum, Pennsylvania. Bainton was memorable as the guide to Luther—his unique voice and white hair, bringing the reformer vibrantly to life.

During my last year in high school, I read Bainton's classic, *Here I Stand: A Life of Martin Luther*. Bainton again brought Luther alive in vivid ways, as a reformer and theologian who knew the terror—as well as the graciousness—of Almighty God. Fifteen years later, I met Bainton while I was teaching theology at the University of Dubuque Theological Seminary, and he signed my book. It is a treasured possession.

Dr. Jack Rogers, my religion professor at Westminster College, New Wilmington, Pennsylvania, introduced me further to Luther in his course on Christian doctrine. Jack brings a clarity and passion to all he communicates, and he fueled my Luther interest. I wrote a paper for the class titled "The Doctrine of Grace in Martin Luther's Theology." So I was able to dip into Luther on a scholarly level.

Through the years as a theologian, pastor, and editor, I wrote pieces on Luther and learned appreciatively from him. I was grateful to propose and be the editor for *The Cambridge Companion to Martin Luther* (Cambridge University Press, 2003). This book immersed me further in Luther scholarship and enabled me to enlist and work with outstanding Luther scholars to produce the volume.

For this devotional book, I express appreciation to a fine Luther scholar and my friend Dr. Deanna A. Thompson of Hamline University in St. Paul, Minnesota. Deanna's book, *Crossing the Divide: Luther, Feminism, and the Cross* (Fortress Press, 2004) is a splendid study. She was gracious in reading these devotions, suggesting some tweaking and nuancing—and helping the pieces maintain a fidelity to Luther. I am most grateful for her help and our friendship through the years.

I want to thank David Dobson of Westminster John Knox Press for helping this project move ahead; and to two of the truly great production persons in publishing, Julie Tonini and Dan Braden. These three of my former colleagues are fine friends and outstanding professionals.

This book, as all my other writing, owes more than I can express to my wonderful family. My wife, LindaJo, is the one with whom I share life's deepest joys. She blesses me. Our son Stephen, his wife, Caroline, and their daughters, Maddie and Annie, are our delights as are our son Karl and his wife, Lauren. For the blessings of our family, I am profoundly grateful.

The book is dedicated to my friend and pastor, Rev. John Michael Krech of Grace Presbyterian Church of Bartlett, Tennessee. We share a mutual love of theology as well as that grand old game that also brings happiness to life—baseball! Mike is a respected pastor, preacher, and friend. I am thankful for his ministries, our friendship, and delightful times together.

Believing
as a Christian

1. The Manger in Which Christ Lies

Think of the Scriptures as the loftiest and noblest of holy things, as the richest of mines which can never be sufficiently explored, in order that you may find that divine wisdom which God here lays before you in such simple guise as to quench all pride. Here you will find the swaddling cloths and the manger in which Christ lies, and to which the angel points the shepherds [Luke 2:12]. Simple and lowly are these swaddling cloths, but dear is the treasure, Christ, who lies in them. (*LW* 35:236)

Martin Luther was a man immersed in Holy Scripture. In his various roles — as a theologian, preacher, teacher, biblical commentator, biblical translator, and all else — Luther was absorbed and deeply occupied with the study of the Bible.

Luther dealt with the Bible on a number of levels. He was concerned with the words of the biblical text as he translated the Old and New Testaments. He desired to hear what the writers of Scripture meant when they wrote. He wanted to understand the theological teachings of Scripture And he was passionate to proclaim the message of Scripture.

In it all, Luther believed the Bible presented God's divine wisdom, given through ordinary writers. Supremely, the Bible presents Jesus Christ. As the shepherds were pointed to the manger by the angels at Jesus' birth, so we are pointed by the Scriptures as the "swaddling cloths" and manger that hold the treasure of God's Son.

The Scriptures center in Jesus Christ, our Lord and Savior. As we study and seek to understand the Bible, we keep Christ in front of us. We thank God for the Scriptures as the manger in which Christ lies.

2. The Book of God's Promises

> So you see that the gospel is really not a book of laws
> and commandments which requires deeds of us, but a
> book of divine promises in which God promises, offers,
> and gives us all his possessions and benefits in Christ.
> (*LW* 35:120)

What is the Bible? There are many views about what the Bible
is and how we should understand it. Throughout our culture,
people refer to the Bible in different ways. They decide whether
or not this ancient book has any importance or relevance for us
today.

Some people see the Bible in a negative light. It is a book
with many laws and commandments to restrict and regulate
human life.

But for Luther, the Bible is not about God trying to tell people what to do in order to gain favor with God or meet God's
requirements. It is not about what we can do for God. It has a
bigger purpose. The Bible is about what God does for us. The
Bible is a book of divine promises. It tells us what God promises
to do, now and in the future. Here we find what God wants to
give and share with us.

This book of God's promises tells us what God offers and
gives us in Jesus Christ. In Christ, we receive a life with benefits like none other. It is a life that can come from no other
source. God's promises provide the riches of God through what
Jesus Christ has done for us. Christ brings God's love and salvation. In Christ, God is with us. The fullness of God's loving
presence is ours in Christ. This is the most important benefit we
can ever imagine!

3. Trinity

So we, too, have our being in God, move and live in Him (Acts 17:28). We have our being because of the Father, who is the "Substance" of the Godhead. We are moved by the image of the Son, who, moved by a divine and eternal motion, so to speak, is born of the Father. We live according to the Spirit, in whom the Father and the Son rest and live, as it were. But these matters are too sublime to belong here. (*LW* 27:290)

Our lives are grounded in the Holy Trinity. We owe the origins of who we are and who we can become in Jesus Christ, to the one God: Father, Son, and Holy Spirit.

The Trinity is a basic of Christian belief. The God revealed in Jesus Christ and made known to us by the Holy Spirit is one God. God is one; but God is three persons. These three are eternal, sharing one "substance" or essence or being. They are three distinct "persons" who are active in the world—and in our lives—as Scripture proclaims.

In interpreting Paul's words: "And because you are children, God has sent the Spirit of his Son into our hearts, crying 'Abba! Father!'" (Gal. 4:6), Luther recognizes what the church came to believe is the work of the triune God in bringing us to become children of God.

Each of the three persons is involved in our lives of faith. The full Trinity brings salvation to us. How this occurs is a sublime mystery. The Trinity is not an abstract doctrine to baffle us. It is the reality of our lives, as created by God and as adopted into the family of God as God's children. Praise the Holy Trinity!

4. God Creates All Things

It is God who creates, effects, and preserves all things through his almighty power and right hand, as our Creed confesses. For he dispatches no officials or angels when he creates or preserves something, but all this is the work of his divine power itself. (*LW* 37:57)

God creates and is continuously active in creation. This was basic for Luther. God brought all things into existence and continues creatively to support and preserve all God has made.

In this, Luther affirmed what the ancient creeds confess. In the familiar words of the Apostles' Creed: "I believe in God, the Father almighty, maker [creator] of heaven and earth." The origin of all things is with God. However God chose to create, it is God's power that is the source of all. In trying to capture the greatness of this power, Luther said it is "uncircumscribed and immeasurable, beyond and above all that is or may be." We can imagine nothing and no power greater than is ascribed to almighty God. There is no need for any intermediary to accomplish God's creative purposes, says Luther. It is all the work of God's divine power itself.

Two important things follow from Luther's convictions here. First, we owe our origins to God. As Luther affirmed in his Small Catechism: "I believe that God has created me together with all that exists."[1] God is our creator. Second, God's presence is real and exists everywhere in the created order. Everywhere we can be, God is with us!

5. "God Is Nothing Else than Love"

Indeed, God is nothing else than love. For even though He is also goodness, yet all His blessings flow from love. These words are of great importance, and they are believed by few, yes, by very few. For the most part we look at God with a sad and hard heart, and we regard Him as a Judge. Therefore he who is imbued with the knowledge that God is love is happy. (*LW* 30:300)

One of the simplest, yet most profound definitions of God is in 1 John 4:16: "God is love." No description says so much in just three words!

In commenting on this verse, Luther makes comprehensive claims that "God is nothing else than love." This means love is the basic reality of God that from which all else flows. Luther indicates that while it is true God is "also goodness," yet, all God's blessings "flow from love." "God is good" is true of God. But when it comes to indicating the source of the blessings God gives to the world—and to each of us, Luther attributes these to God's most basic characteristic: God is love.

Yet not everyone believes this. Indeed, Luther thought this is believed by "very few." Our view of God is more likely a view that produces "a sad and hard heart." This is when God is regarded as a Judge. Certainly Luther believed the Scriptures teach that God is a judge. Judgment is a dimension of God's actions.

But there is more and a better view. For "God is nothing else than love." This reverses sadness and hardness of heart. To know that God is love brings happiness. It is our deepest joy! What better news can there be?!

6. God in the Shame of the Cross

Now it is not sufficient for anyone, and it does him no good to recognize God in his glory and majesty, unless he recognizes him in the humility and shame of the cross. Thus God destroys the wisdom of the wise, as Isa. [45:15] says, "Truly, thou art a God who hidest thyself." (*LW* 31:52)

In theological theses prepared for the *Heidelberg Disputation* (1518), the young Luther laid out his emerging theology. He distinguished two approaches, between a "theology of glory" and a "theology of the cross."

Luther characterized the dominant theology of his day as a "theology of the glory," which sought to know of God's invisible nature through speculating on God's divine power and wisdom, through God's works in creation (see Rom. 1:20–23). This could lead persons to think that they are "worthy and wise."

But for Luther, this misses the fact that humans are sinful and now must know the true God only in relation to their sin and God's divine judgment. They must know God through a "theology of the cross," where God is both hidden and revealed in Jesus Christ. God is hidden in what the world considers "foolish" (1 Cor. 1:25), in Jesus' humanity, weakness, and suffering. Luther put it starkly: "God can be found only in suffering and the cross" (*LW* 31:53).

Faith recognizes God in the shame and suffering of Christ on the cross. Theology is about salvation and not about philosophical ideas. We encounter the true God in the man Jesus, who as the Son of God, suffered as the means to the gift of salvation — unattainable through human reason, good works, or ethical actions. The "wisdom of the wise" is destroyed.

7. Adoring Ourselves as an Idol

But this is completely wrong, namely to please oneself, to enjoy oneself in one's works, and to adore oneself as an idol. He who is self-confident and without fear of God, however, acts entirely in this manner. For if he had fear he would not be self-confident, and for this reason he would not be pleased with himself, but he would be pleased with God. (*LW* 31:46)

In discussing the First Commandment (Exod. 20:3) in his Large Catechism, Luther said that "anything on which your heart relies and depends, I say, that is really your God." For "to have a god is nothing else than to trust and believe in that one with your whole heart."[2]

This is human sin. To trust and depend on something other than God is to have an "idol." The First Commandment is God's prohibition of idols, which Luther sees in his Heidelberg Disputation as including "to enjoy oneself in one's works, and to adore oneself as an idol."

This is so basic—and so easy—to fall into as a way of life. No wonder idolatry is taken up in the First Commandment! Making an idol of one's self—"self-adoration"—is there. It is the sinful inclination that lurks within us all. We rely and depend on many things: our wealth, status, power, or social position. These, we believe, will bring us the security and celebrity we crave—living in the "spotlight." They become "gods," idols.

But our hearts are truly to rely on God. We trust and depend and cling to God alone!

8. Turned In on Ourselves

Scripture [Isa. 2:9–22] . . . describes man as so turned in on himself that he uses not only physical but even spiritual goods for his own purposes and in all things seeks only himself. This curvedness is now natural for us, a natural wickedness and a natural sinfulness. Thus man has no help from his natural powers, but he needs the aid of some power outside of himself. (*LW* 25:345)

Vividly, Luther described sinful humans as "curved in" on themselves (Lat. *in curvatus in se*). This is a basic idolatry of depending on the self instead of God. It is "self-seeking" instead of "God-seeking." It is our "natural wickedness," says Luther, our "natural sinfulness."

Luther traces this to "the viciousness of original sin," humanity's sinfulness in its origins. This infects us now as what Scripture calls "curvedness, iniquity and crookedness" (*LW* 25:313).

Like others, we are self-absorbed, seeking our own purposes. We have a gnawing anxiety—as Luther himself did—that we are not good enough before God; so we want to justify ourselves. This insecurity and anxiety fuels our self-preoccupation. We are desperate to know what we can do to make ourselves right with God. So we look in a "mirror" at ourselves, instead of out a "window" in care and concern for others—and for God.

Bound this way, we have "no help" from our "natural powers." We need "the aid of some power outside" ourselves. Our self-serving propensities, driven by anxieties, do not let us escape their clutches. Our "curvedness" constrains us; we need a power beyond our own to transform us and turn our lives in new directions. We need the power of God!

9. The Law as Mirror

Thus the Law serves to indicate the will of God, and it leads us to a realization that we cannot keep it. It also acquaints us with the nature of man, with his capabilities, and with his limitations. The Law was given to us for the revelation of sin; but it does not have the power to save us from sin and rid us of it. It holds a mirror before us; we peer into it and perceive that we are devoid of righteousness and life. And this image impels us to cry: "Oh, come, Lord Jesus Christ, help us and give us grace to enable us to fulfill the Law's demands!" (*LW* 22:143)

Luther had much to say about the law of God. The law was given by God to the people of Israel to let them know how they were to live to be in obedience to their Lord.

But this gift of God showed the people how far short they fell of obeying God. It revealed their sin and that they are "judged by the law" (Rom. 2:12). So sinful people see, as Luther says, that "we cannot keep" the law. Our human nature is sinful, idolatrous; and so the law does not have the power to save us and "rid us" of sin. For the law "holds a mirror before us; we peer into it and perceive that we are devoid of righteousness and life." The law shows us we are not the people we should be.

Confronted by our sinfulness in the face of God's law, we have no hope. We can only cry for help from the Lord Jesus Christ, says Luther: "Help us and give us grace"! Grace is found only in Christ.

10. The Law as Hammer

This is what finally happens to all self-righteous people who are drunk with the presumption of their own
righteousness. They think that when there is no trouble,
they are the dearly beloved of God, and that God has
regard for their vows, fasts, little prayers, and alms and
will grant them a special crown in heaven in exchange
for these. But when thunder and lightning come out of
the blue, the fire and hammer that smashes rocks, that
is, the Law of God that reveals sin and that shows the
wrath and judgment of God, they are driven to despair.
(*LW* 26:312)

Many folks think they are pretty decent people. They exhibit
the characteristics of "good people," being upstanding citizens
and living their lives in ways acceptable to others—and even to
God. If they need any measure of "righteousness," it is stored up
within themselves.

For Luther, this is a totally mistaken view. He recognized
there are "self-righteous people who are drunk with the presumption of their own righteousness." They may perform
religious works, even "vows, fasts, little prayers, and alms,"
which they hope will "grant them a special crown in heaven in
exchange for these."

Yet things are not so good. God's law, like "thunder and
lightning come out of the blue." It reveals sin and shows those
trusting their self-righteousness that God's wrath and judgment are upon them. The law is like "the fire and hammer that
smashes rocks." All self-righteousness is shattered. All works
to gain God's favor are crushed. The law is a hammer that can
bring only despair.

But it is only when there is total despair of doing anything to
gain God's favor by one's self, that another word of God can be
heard: Gospel!

11. Sin and Its Consequences

A total lack of uprightness and of the power of all the faculties both of body and soul and of the whole inner and outer man. On top of all this, it is a propensity toward evil. It is a nausea toward the good, a loathing of light and wisdom, and a delight in error and darkness, a flight from and an abomination of all good works, a pursuit of evil [Ps. 14:3; Gen. 8:21]. (*LW* 25:299)

The effects of human sin are damaging and far-reaching. Sin is revealed by the law of God and drives us to despair.

Luther traces this to "original sin." It is sin derived from the disobedience of humanity's first parents (Adam and Eve—Gen. 3). It is passed on to all humans as a "total lack of uprightness" and a "propensity toward evil." This hereditary sinfulness expresses itself in unbelief in God and in humanity's "curvedness"—the love of self; and reliance on "temporal goods and other created things more than on its Creator." Sin is "the pursuit of evil." "Everyone," said Luther, "is so inclined" (*LW* 68:55).

Effects of sin are a rupture of the relationship of love and trust God intends. There is loss of fellowship and righteousness before God. Sin places humans as guilty in the face of the law of God.

There is only one hope: "However much the Law may accuse me, and sin and death may terrify me, nevertheless Thou, O God, dost promise grace, righteousness, and eternal life through Christ." And so the promise produces the sigh that cries: "Father!" (*LW* 26:389).

12. No Free Will, except to Do Evil

We do not have free will, except to choose what is evil.
(*LW* 68:39)

For Luther, humans are so pervaded by sin that the human will is not free to choose to obey and follow God.

Luther's important work, *De servo arbitrio* (*The Bondage of the Will* [1525]), dealt with this. It responded to the great humanist scholar, Desiderius Erasmus (1466?–1536), who wrote *De libero arbitrio diatribe sive collatio* (*A Diatribe or Discourse concerning Free Choice* [1524]). Erasmus defined "free choice" as "a power of the human will by which a man can apply himself to the things which lead to eternal salvation, or turn away from them."[3]

To Luther, this would mean humans can cooperate in their salvation. But sin has radically corrupted reasoning and willing. In a sermon, Luther put it succinctly: "We do not have free will, except to choose what is evil."

Daily we worship what is not God; we are preoccupied with ourselves and don't seek God's will. Humans, sinful by nature, will always choose in accord with their nature, their sinful wills preventing them from obeying God's law and will. Their wills will evil. Luther preached, "It is impossible to be saved by human ability or powers. God's hand must reach in. He must set the human heart in order again and occupy it" (*LW* 68:55). Gratefully, God does, in Jesus Christ, by the power of the Holy Spirit.

13. Son of God and Son of Mary

He is the only-begotten Son of God and is already the Son before He is born of Mary. This is the twofold birth of Christ. First, there is the birth by which He is called God's Son. This birth is from eternity. This same one wanted to be a mother hen and was with all the prophets. Afterward He became a man, was born of Mary, and yet they are not two but only one Son. (*LW* 68:250)

Jesus Christ is the center of Christian faith. As the eternal Son of God who became a human being, Jesus conveys God's love. In his life, death, and resurrection he provides salvation for sinful humanity. Jesus does for sinners what we cannot do for ourselves: forgives sin and reconciles us with God in a relationship of love and trust.

Luther affirmed what the early church believed about who Jesus was: "Christ is God and man in one person. He has neither sinned nor died, and is not condemned, and he cannot sin, die, or be condemned; his righteousness, life, and salvation are unconquerable, eternal, omnipotent" (*LW* 31:351). Only the sinless, righteous Son of God saves those whose sins condemn them.

Jesus Christ is both "Son of God and Son of Mary." He is one person with two natures: divine and human. Both are necessary for salvation to be achieved. Jesus Christ was "already the Son before He is born of Mary" since he is the eternal second person of the Trinity, the "only-begotten Son of God." He became a human in his birth to Mary. He shares in our human condition, except for sin. This is the Christ who saves us!

14. King Jesus

This is quite a wonderful description of this King. Just as He is very different from all the kings of the world, so also His area of responsibility and His royal apparatus are clearly different from those which fit a king of this world. Here there is no violence, no armor, no power, no anger, no wrath. All these, you see, are proper for kings of this world. Here there are only kindness, justice, salvation, mercy, and every good thing. In short, He dispenses the sweetness and the mercy of God. He is just, because He justifies. He is Savior, because He saves. (*LW* 20:94)

On Palm Sunday, Jesus rode into Jerusalem to the cheers of the crowd (Matt. 21:1–11). Gospel writers saw this event as a fulfillment of the prophecy of Zechariah 9:9 (Matt. 21:5; John 12:15).

Here, King Jesus is shown as a king who is "very different," says Luther, "from all the kings of the world." The contrast with a king of this world is overwhelming. Kings of this world (in Luther's view) are justified in using the sword and carrying out the responsibilities of government, which can include violence and war.

But in King Jesus, there is "no violence, no armor, no power, no anger, no wrath." Jesus' kingship is of a different order. His is a spiritual kingdom, marked by "only kindness, justice, salvation, mercy, and every good thing." These are characteristics of the kind of king Jesus is. "In short," said Luther, "he dispenses the sweetness and the mercy of God." In himself, Jesus embodies these spiritual realities.

"Kindness, justice, salvation, mercy, and every good thing" are in King Jesus. He comes in humility, in peace, and brings us what we most need.

15. Jesus Humbled Himself for Me

We are told that He was weak, that He was like any other man in body and soul, that He made Himself subject to all human infirmities, that He hungered and thirsted, that He experienced all the wants of flesh and blood. In this weakness the true and eternal God shows Himself. For me He humbles Himself; and for me He is finally crucified, although He is at the same time very God, who redeems me from sin and death. (*LW* 22:507)

The man Jesus was just like us, except for sin. Luther is clear that Jesus was "like any other man in body and soul, that He made Himself subject to all human infirmities, that He hungered and thirsted, that He experienced all the wants of flesh and blood." Luther said Jesus "assumes worry, weakness, and fear. He acts like a real man." This is a full identification with us humans, as we are.

In this, Jesus displayed "weakness." He took on human flesh and experience; and did so as the "true and eternal God." So God shows who God is, not in the glories of heaven—but in the "stuff" of human life, on earth—in the man, Jesus. This is where the true God is found.

The absolutely amazing benefit is that God has humbled himself in the man Jesus—"for me" (cf. Gal. 2:20). Jesus who was "at the same time very God" (see the Nicene Creed) died and "redeems me from sin and death." No one else could bring this salvation.

The crucified God was crucified, for me! Jesus' death has the power to save us because he was "very God." In his humility, Jesus died for the world (John 3:16), for all—including me.

16. Christ Bears Our Sins

And this is our highest comfort, to clothe and wrap
Christ this way in my sins, your sins, and the sins of the
entire world, and in this way to behold Him bearing all
our sins. (*LW* 26:279)

Luther often referred to the death of Jesus Christ. He used
many images to reflect biblical descriptions of Jesus' death on
the cross and its effects for salvation.

Jesus took upon himself what we sinners deserve. Jesus, the
sinless Son of God, suffered and died for us who deserve the
"wages of sin," which is "death" (Rom. 6:23). Jesus is "the man
who stepped into the place of our sinful nature" (*LW* 76:19). We
cannot "be obedient to God or fulfil the law," so Jesus became
"obedient in place of all of us or for the sake of all of us" (*LW*
34:119). He "took all our sins upon Himself, and for them He
died on the cross" (*LW* 26:277).

The church has never said there is only one correct way to
understand how the death of Christ brings salvation. No single
"theory of the atonement" can say it all. In two examples, Luther
said Christ made "eternal satisfaction for our sin and reconciles
us with God the Father" (*LW* 51:92; cf. *LW* 26:277). Christ also
died to "avert from us the wrath of God" (*LW* 36:177).

However we understand it, we find "this is our highest comfort, to clothe and wrap Christ this way in my sins."

17. Beautiful, Glorious Exchange

Is not this a beautiful, glorious exchange, by which Christ, who is wholly innocent and holy, not only takes upon himself another's sin, that is, my sin and guilt, but also clothes and adorns me, who am nothing but sin, with his own innocence and purity? (*LW* 51:316)

Jesus Christ in his death on the cross brings salvation. Our sin is forgiven, and we receive the gift of reconciliation with the God against whom we have sinned. Those sins, which accuse our conscience, which reveal our alienation, and the law, which stands against us as an accuser, now — in Jesus Christ — have no power over us. They have no reality since Christ has brought us into God's favor. As Luther put it, "When we see that [our sins] lie on Christ, and He has overcome them through His resurrection, and we boldly believe this, then they are dead and come to nothing" (*LW* 76:430). This is glorious liberation and release! The past is over and gone! Life is new!

This is possible through a "beautiful, glorious exchange" between Christ and us. As Luther put it, "Christ, who is wholly innocent and holy, not only takes upon himself another's sin, that is, my sin and guilt, but also clothes and adorns me, who am nothing but sin, with his own innocence and purity." The sinless One becomes sin; and the sinner becomes righteous (2 Cor. 5:21).

When we consider the magnitude of salvation, how great it is and how utterly impossible it would be to attain it by ourselves, we are staggered that Christ died for us. We are overcome with gratitude, joy, and praise!

18. Christ Is Risen!

Cling with a firm faith to the fact that your Christ has risen from the dead. He, too, suffered such anguish and fear of hell, but through His resurrection He has overcome all. Therefore, even though I am a sinner and deserving of death and hell, this shall nonetheless be my consolation and my victory that my Lord Jesus lives and has risen so that He, in the end, might rescue me from sin, death, and hell. (*LW* 28:105)

The death of Jesus Christ is made effective through Christ's glorious resurrection. Luther saw the resurrection of Jesus Christ as central to Christian doctrine, even calling it "the chief article of our faith" (*LW* 30:12).

The humiliation of Jesus, his suffering and anguish on the cross, and his God-forsakenness (Mark 15:34) is the worst pain imaginable. It marked the deepest torment. All this for the innocent Son of God. Luther even believed Jesus suffered a "fear of hell."

But Christ is risen! His resurrection "has overcome all." Now and in the future, "Christ is Risen!" changes our existence. As Paul says, notes Luther, "the victory gained by Christ . . . will completely do away with and purge our sin and death with its attendant frailties, perils, and sufferings of the body." By faith we believe "Christ's resurrection is our resurrection" (*LW* 28:202).

Sinners deserving "death and hell" have been consoled. We have been given the victory of the risen Christ so "He, in the end, might rescue me from sin, death, and hell." The Lord is risen! He is risen indeed!

19. Christ Is Everywhere

> Christ's body is everywhere because it is at the right hand of God which is everywhere, although we do not know how that occurs. For we also do not know how it occurs that the right hand of God is everywhere. (*LW* 37:214)

The resurrection of Jesus Christ was followed by his ascension into heaven. This completed Christ's life on earth. He now shares the glorified life of the second person of the Trinity in heaven. As Luther said, "He has brought Himself to completion to the point of fullness of divine essence by ascending into heaven" (*LW* 25:147).

Jesus is "seated at the right hand" of God, as the Creed confesses. Luther interpreted "the right hand of God" to mean that Christ is everywhere, because "the right hand of God" is everywhere. Thus, Christ's body now, in his glorified human nature, is infinite and present in all places. This is called ubiquity. Luther said we cannot understand how this occurs. But it does. On this Luther would not relent.

The issue was of particular importance in Reformation controversies over the nature of the Lord's Supper. Against Huldrych Zwingli (1484–1531) and John Calvin (1509–1564), representatives of the Reformed theological tradition, Luther maintained Christ is present everywhere and in all celebrations of the Lord's Supper, by the power of the Holy Spirit. This is possible by the union of Christ's human nature with the divine person of the Word (Logos). This focused on the presence of Jesus Christ in the Lord's Supper.

In a nonsacramental context, Christ is everywhere means that we are never outside the presence of Christ. No situation or event can keep Christ from being with us and surrounding us with Christ's love.

20. Christic in the Lord's Supper

We must always bear with one another. . . . Christ has
not only portrayed that to us by His own example and
presented it by His Word, but He has also depicted it in
the form of the Sacrament, namely, in bread and wine.
We hold that under the bread and wine are the true body
and blood of Christ, even as it is. Here we see one thing
and believe another, which portrays faith. . . . So also love
is portrayed in these signs and forms. (*LW* 76:447–48)

Reformation controversies about the Lord Supper focused on
the presence of Christ in the sacrament. This issue divided Protestant Christians.

Luther's view is sometimes called consubstantiation (a medi-
eval term), which some Luther scholars question. Luther says
that "under the bread and wine are the true body and blood of
Christ." He did not believe in a change in the "substance" of the
bread and wine, as in the Roman Catholic view of transubstan-
tiation. For Luther, the body and blood of Christ coexist or are
conjoined in union with each other: bread with body; and wine
with blood. This is analogous to the union of the two natures in
the person of Christ. In the Supper, Jesus Christ is present and
binds his presence to the sacrament in the elements of bread
and wine. This is a unique and altogether special instance of the
presence of Christ.

Here, faith is required, because one thing is "seen" and
another thing is "believed." Here, "love is portrayed in these
signs and forms." Here, "body and blood are given in order
that we whose sins are forgiven us may have salvation!" (*LW*
36:176).

21. The Holy Spirit Brings Us to Christ

Neither you nor I could ever know anything about Christ, or believe in him and receive him as Lord, unless these were offered to us and bestowed on our heart through the preaching of the gospel by the Holy Spirit. . . . God has caused the Word to be published and proclaimed, in which he has given the Holy Spirit to offer and apply to us this treasure, this redemption.[4]

Establishing faith in Jesus Christ is by the work of the Holy Spirit. The Spirit brings faith through the Word and is active in the sanctification of Christian believers, their growth in holiness.

The human will, captive to the power of sin, can be changed only by the Spirit's work. The Spirit of God applies the Word of God—in Scripture and preaching—to the hearts of sinners. The gift of faith is given, and the sinner's will is made free to love and obey God through faith in Jesus Christ. The Holy Spirit is given "to offer and apply to us this treasure, this redemption," said Luther.

The Spirit works through the preaching of the gospel. Human reason cannot bring faith. For Luther, "The Spirit, and no one else, can bring the Lord to mind" (*LW* 19:79). The Spirit works through the Word, not as "sectarian" opponents said, "without the Word." The Spirit can effectively call to mind and enkindle faith in our hearts, "even though it [the Word] has not been heard for ten years" (*LW* 14:62). Praise God the Holy Spirit!

22. Grace Is God's Favor

> I take grace in the proper sense of the favor of God—
> not a quality of the soul, as is taught by our more recent
> writers. This grace truly produces peace of heart until
> finally a man is healed from his corruption and feels he
> has a gracious God. (*LW* 32:227)

In some ways, the Protestant Reformation was a controversy over the nature of God's grace and how it is received.

Luther's basic definition of grace is "the favor of God." This indicates the relational nature of grace. When God relates to humans in a way that shows divine favor, instead of judgment or destruction, there is grace. In contrast to the scholastic theology of the times, which had highly developed distinctions about differences in "grace," Luther's concept was simpler. God's grace did not, for example, create a capacity in humans to be able to fulfill God's law. It did not produce a "quality of the soul" that enabled humans to earn merit.

Instead, for Luther, God's grace is given in freedom by God and provides for the justification of the sinner in Jesus Christ. God sends Jesus Christ and provides the means by which the divine favor is given. It is, as Luther said, "grace, without merit or works" and "this grace is not given except through the redemption which is in Christ Jesus" (*LW* 25:31). Grace is focused in Christ. God's grace "bestows the remission of sins" through Christ (*LW* 25:6). This is the sole way of redemption and new life.

Grace in Christ "produces peace of heart." Peace comes because we are "healed" from our "corruption." Now, a "gracious God"—which Luther himself sought—is found!

23. Absolved for Christ's Sake

God can do this, that though sin remains, he considers us to be righteous and pure, and that a man is so absolved, as if he had no sin, for Christ's sake. We truly thank God, because his imputation is greater than our impurity. And sin, which in substance is not being removed, shall be imputed as having been removed and shall be absorbed by the goodness of God who conceals it on account of Christ who overshadows it, although it remains in nature and substance. (*LW* 34:166)

God's grace in salvation is expressed through the way salvation is received by sinful persons. By the Holy Spirit, sinners are justified by faith.

Succinctly, Luther said, "the term 'to be justified' means that a man is considered righteous" (*LW* 34:167). More fully, God forgives and absolves sin, treating the sinner as if one "had no sin, for Christ's sake." God accepts Christ's righteousness as covering sin or in place of the sinner's sin. So, "his righteousness is yours; your sin is His" (*LW* 26:233).

This is called imputation. Christ's righteousness is imputed to us, and we are considered righteous in God's sight. We are righteous "solely by the imputation of God and not of ourselves or of our own works . . . our righteousness is not something in us or in our power" (*LW* 25:257). Since Christ's righteousness comes from outside ourselves, Luther calls it "alien righteousness" (see *LW* 34:178 and *LW* 31:299).

Yet Christ's righteousness "becomes truly ours" (*LW* 24:347). For which we "truly thank God" (*LW* 34:166).

24. Justification by Faith

Where the confidence of the heart is present, therefore, there Christ is present, in that very cloud and faith. This is the formal righteousness on account of which a man is justified. . . . The Christ who is grasped by faith and who lives in the heart is the true Christian righteousness, on account of which God counts us righteous and grants us eternal life. (*LW* 26:130)

God's imputation of Christ's righteousness in justification is like a legal act in which the sinner is declared righteous. So Luther's view is called forensic. For Luther, justification by faith is a central Christian teaching. It is "the chief article of our Christian doctrine, that we are justified before God only through faith in Christ" (*LW* 68:104).

In justification, Christ is received with faith, by the grace of God. Faith is the form by which we receive Christ. Christ can be received no other way; faith is the only way Christ can give himself to us. It is through believing that God "justifies, that is, [God] accounts people righteous" (*LW* 25:205).

Faith is a matter of the mind, but also of the heart, for Luther. Faith is a "confidence of the heart," and Christ "lives in the heart." Said Luther, "faith justifies because it takes hold of and possesses this treasure, the present Christ." This is a most personal and intimate appropriation of our Savior. Indeed, "true faith with arms outstretched joyfully embraces the Son of God given for it and says, 'He is my beloved and I am his'" (*LW* 34:110). We embrace Christ!

25. Righteous and Sinner at the Same Time

Now, is he perfectly righteous? No, for he is at the same time both a sinner and a righteous man; a sinner in fact, but a righteous man by the sure imputation and promise of God that He will continue to deliver him from sin until He has completely cured him. And thus he is entirely healthy in hope, but in fact he is still a sinner; but he has the beginning of righteousness, so that he continues more and more always to seek it, yet he realizes that he is always unrighteous. (*LW* 25:260)

Luther's view of the Christian as justified by faith does not mean Christians become "perfect" or sinless people. One of the famous sayings associated with Luther is that the Christian believer is *simul justus et peccator* — "at the same time righteous and a sinner." The Christian is "holy and profane, an enemy of God and a child of God" (*LW* 26:232).

This double character remains the self-identity of the Christian from the experience of faith until final glory, when all sin will be removed and we are, as Luther says, "cured." It is a great paradox of Christian existence. Christians are simultaneously righteous and sinners. We are righteous in Jesus Christ and sinners in ourselves. Human logic or reason cannot handle this description — it is contradictory. But the reality is that Christians are just and sinners, at the same time. We are both, completely.

While God's grace enables the Christian to do good works, Christians also stand in daily need of forgiveness. We have, says Luther, "the beginning of righteousness," so we continue to seek it. Yet, we sin and realize we are "always unrighteous."

26. Good Works

"Good works do not make a good man, but a good man does good works; evil works do not make a wicked man, but a wicked man does evil works." Consequently it is always necessary that the substance or person himself be good before there can be any good works, and that good works follow and proceed from the good person. (*LW* 31:361)

The issue of "works" was always present for Luther. Doing "good works" or obedience to God's law is not possible for sinners because of the devastating effects of sin on the human will and desires.

But for Christians, who have been justified by faith, good works in God's sight are possible. While Luther's motto for salvation was *sola fide*—by "faith alone," for Luther, justifying faith will never be "alone." Good works will follow justification. The life of the Christian is the continuing growth in holiness or sanctification. This includes good works that serve God by serving others. These become signs, not causes of justification. As Luther famously put it: "Good works do not make a good [justified] person, but a good person does good works." Or, "works are necessary to salvation, but they do not cause salvation, because faith alone gives life" (*LW* 34:165).

Good works can never be a basis for salvation or a "badge of achievement" to bring before God as "merit." Instead, good works proceed from faith and the power of the Holy Spirit to express the genuineness of one's faith in Jesus Christ.

Works accompany faith as the expression of the nature of our Christian faith to be shown in loving others. As Luther colorfully put it, ours is "a faith which is powerfully active, not one that snores once it has been 'acquired'" (*LW* 27:336).

27. One Holy Christian Church

> I believe that there is one holy Christian Church on
> earth, i.e. the community or number or assembly of all
> Christians in all the world, the one bride of Christ, and
> his spiritual body of which he is the only head. (*LW*
> 37:367)

Luther lived his faith in the context of the church. His controversies with the Roman Catholic Church led him to think deeply
about what constitutes the true church and its true nature. So
ecclesiology, the doctrine of the church, was very important to
Luther.

At its basic level, in the face of the established Roman Church,
Luther proclaimed the creedal affirmation: I believe in "the holy
Christian [Apostles' Creed: 'catholic'] church." The Christian
church on earth is "the community or number or assembly of
all Christians." Christian believers constitute the Christian community. These together are "the one bride of Christ"—belong-
ing to Christ—and spreading throughout the world. The church
is a unity, despite its diversities of peoples, places, and struc-
tures. The church's unity is in its head, Jesus Christ. If Christ
is the head of the church, all earthly church leaders must look
to him, as must all Christian believers. As Luther said, "The
bishops or priests are not her heads or lords or bridegrooms, but
servants, friends, and—as the word 'bishop' implies—superin-
tendents, guardians, or stewards." Christ exercises authority in
the church as the Lord of the church.

The church is Christ's "spiritual body." The Holy Spirit
works through the community of believers, drawing the community together on the basis of faith in Jesus Christ. The Christian community is the way the triune God gathers the people
of God to share the gospel of Christ and to be led by the Holy
Spirit.

28. The Communion of Saints

> The creed clearly indicates what the church is, namely, a communion of saints, that is, a crowd [Hauffe] assembly of people who are Christians and holy, which is called a Christian holy assembly, or church. (*LW* 41:143)

The phrase "communion of saints" in the Apostles' Creed defines the nature of the church. The communion, says Luther, is "a crowd assembly of people"—that is, a corporate body—"who are Christians and holy" joined in common faith in Jesus Christ and who are "called a Christian holy assembly, or church"; the communion is marked by holiness, a focused dedication to being the people of God.

"Communion" (Greek *koinōnia*) is a rich term that can also be translated "fellowship." The church as the "fellowship of all saints" is, said Luther, where "we are all brothers and sisters, so closely united that a closer relationship cannot be conceived. For here we have one baptism, one Christ, one sacrament, one food, one gospel, one faith, one Spirit, one spiritual body [Eph. 4:4–5], and each person is a member of the other [Rom. 12:5]" (*LW* 35:70).

This captures the richness of the communion and fellowship that marks the life of the Christian community. This relational community unites diverse people in a relationship that is grounded in our unity in Jesus Christ. The communion of saints with each other is an expression of the communion of saints with the "one baptism, one Christ, one sacrament, one food, one gospel, one faith, one Spirit, one spiritual body," which is shared by the whole church. The church's communion is a theological fellowship expressing the church's unity with its Lord. Church is where "each person is a member of the other," bound together by Jesus Christ.

29. God's Word and God's People

God's word cannot be without God's people, and conversely, God's people cannot be without God's word. Otherwise, who would preach or hear it preached, if there were no people of God? And what could or would God's people believe, if there were no word of God? (*LW* 41:150)

The Word of God is active and brings effects. Through the Holy Spirit, the Word establishes the people of God. The people of God—the church—lives by God's ongoing Word to the community. The interrelation between God's Word and God's people is strong.

This is captured by Luther's comment that "God's word cannot be without God's people, and conversely, God's people cannot be without God's word." For him, the church owes its birth to the Word of God in the forms of preaching and the Scriptures. These point to God's revelation in the Word of God, Jesus Christ. God's word continually nourishes, aids, and strengthens the church so "it cannot be without the Word." For "if it is without the Word it ceases to be a church." This means that "a Christian, thus, is born to the ministry of the Word in baptism" (*LW* 40:37). All Christians proclaim the Word of God to express their identity as God's people in Jesus Christ.

The Word, with the sacraments, constitutes the church's identity. Word and sacraments are visible marks of the church. For Luther, "the Church is not seen by outward peace, but by the Word and Sacraments. For wherever you see a little flock that has the Gospel and the Sacraments properly, there is the Church" (*LW* 68:265). Love God's Word and God's people!

30. Church—Holy and Sinner

> They [foolish scholastics] said that the church is holy in the sense that it is completely without sin. The church is indeed holy, but it is a sinner at the same time. Therefore it believes in the forgiveness of sins. . . . Therefore we are not said to be holy formally, as a wall is said to be white because of its inherent whiteness. Our inherent holiness is not enough. Therefore Christ is our entire holiness; where this inherent holiness is not enough, Christ is. (*LW* 26:109)

In the Apostles' Creed, we confess, "I believe in the holy catholic church." That affirmation may be hard to swallow if we have had some bad experiences with the not-so-holy local church!

Luther knew the church was not holy "in the sense that it is completely without sin." The church is "indeed holy, but it is a sinner at the same time." This parallels completely Luther's view of the Christian believer as one who is "at the same time righteous and a sinner" (see above #25). The sinfulness of the church means prayers for forgiveness are always necessary, daily.

So the holiness of the church cannot rest on a "formal" definition, says Luther—"as a wall is said to be white because of its inherent whiteness." "Inherent holiness is not enough," he maintains. That won't work. More is needed.

We look to Jesus Christ. For Luther, "the Church does not depend on the holiness of any [other] person, but alone on the holiness and righteousness of the Lord Christ" (*LW* 68:265–66). Only he. For he is "our entire holiness; where this inherent holiness is not enough, Christ is." So he is!

31. The Church Is Full
of Forgiveness of Sins

> The whole church is full of the forgiveness of sins. But few there are who really accept and receive it. For they do not believe it and would rather rely upon their own works. (*LW* 35:21–22)

Christian experience in the church and our personal lives confirms that while we are justified by faith in Jesus Christ, we are still sinners. Even the "best Christians" are still sinners. If those we respect and honor most as Christian persons are still sinners, then what of us? If gold rusts, what will iron do?

This is why prayers of confession—when the church corporately confesses sin—and personal prayers for forgiveness are constantly necessary. We need forgiveness, always.

The nature of the church and the nature of the God we worship in Jesus Christ is to forgive. When sin occurs, forgiveness is a response. Luther wrote that "in this Christian Church, wherever it exists, is to be found the forgiveness of sins, i.e. a kingdom of grace and of true pardon" (*LW* 37:368). God's reign of grace and pardon should be the nature of what the church does: forgives.

Church practices are means through which forgiveness of sins can become realities. For Luther these included "the gospel, baptism, and the sacrament of the altar, in which the forgiveness of sins is offered, obtained, and received. Moreover, Christ and his Spirit and God are there" (*LW* 37:368). These practices that accompany the forgiving love of other members of the communion of saints provide opportunities for forgiveness to be sought; and received.

Christians cannot "rely upon their own works" in the Christian life. While sin may be "down" within us, it is not "out." Not extinguished. So we really need a whole church full of forgiveness!

32. The Church Will Always Exist

> He gives us the comfort that "a holy Christian Church" will always exist and remain in the world, just as the article of our Creed teaches us. This means that there will always be a little flock, whoever and wherever they may be, who in unity will cling to this Lord, uphold His scepter, and publicly confess His Word. (*LW* 13:285)

At times, we may be tempted to throw in the towel when it comes to the church. Experiences of church difficulties can wound deeply, and we have all known those alienated from the church whose wounds seem not to heal.

Can the church survive through it all—to say nothing of all the cultural challenges and trials and tribulations faced by church bodies and local congregations these days?

Luther believed God helped the church in the past, that Christ has preserved the church, and that God will "help our heirs, to the honor and glory of his divine name forever" (*LW* 47:118). Indeed, "a Christian holy people is to be and to remain on earth until the end of the world. This is an article of faith that cannot be terminated until that which it believes comes, as Christ promises, 'I am with you always, to the close of the age'" [Matt. 28:20] (*LW* 41:148).

No matter what the church faces, Christ's promise is sure. Christ is with us, through to the end. For Luther, "there will always be a little flock, whoever and wherever they may be, who in unity will cling to this Lord, uphold His scepter, and publicly confess His Word." We believe!

33. All Christians Are Priests

It is written in I Pet. 2[:9]: "You are a chosen race, a royal priesthood, and a priestly royalty." Therefore we are all priests, as many of us as are Christians. But the priests, as we call them, are ministers chosen from among us. All that they do is done in our name; the priesthood is nothing but a ministry. This we learn from I Cor. 4[:1]: "This is how one should regard us, as servants of Christ and stewards of the mysteries of God." (*LW* 36:112–13)

The "priesthood of all believers" is associated with Luther. For him, this was derived from the New Testament. Against Roman Catholic hierarchies of church priests, Luther stressed "we are all priests, as many of us as are Christians." "Priests" or "ministers" who serve in the church are carrying out a ministry as "servants of Christ." "The priesthood in the New Testament," said Luther, "is equally in all Christians, in the spirit alone" (*LW* 36:139).

All Christians are priests because it is "faith alone" that is "the true priestly office." Thus, "all Christian men are priests, all women priestesses, be they young or old, master or servant, mistress or maid, learned or unlearned. Here there is no difference, unless faith be unequal" (*LW* 35:101). All believers are equal in Christ.

We look to "one single priest, Christ, who has sacrificed himself for us and all of us with him" (*LW* 36:138). "We need no priest or mediator other than Christ," said Luther, "thus every Christian on his own may pray in Christ and have access to God" (Rom. 5:2) (*LW* 36:138). We pray directly to God through Christ.

34. Food and Drink to Each Other

The fact that we consume one bread and drink makes us to be one bread and drink. And just as one member serves another in such an integrated body, so each one also eats and drinks the other; that is, each consumes the other in everything, and each one is food and drink for the other, so that we are simply food and drink to one another, just as Christ is simply food and drink to us. (*LW* 36:287)

"We Christians," said Luther, "are the spiritual body of Christ and collectively one loaf, one drink, one spirit. All this is achieved by Christ, who through his own body makes us all to be one spiritual body; so that all of us partake equally of his body, and are therefore equal and united with one another" (*LW* 36:286).

The unity of the church which comes from Christ, bonds Christians with one another in Christ's body. This is dramatically represented in the Lord's Supper, where "the fact that we consume one bread and drink makes us to be one bread and drink."

Our bonds with each other in the church, in Christ, are so deep that "each one is food and drink for the other." We are sources of life-giving nourishment to our sisters and brothers in Christ, just as they provide what we need most in life to us.

Put another way, in the church as a community of love, "love engenders love in return and [mutual love] unites" (*LW* 35:51). Our love for one another in the church means participation in the lives of others, in the fellowship (Greek *koinōnia*) of faith. We share ourselves spiritually with one another, loved and being loved.

35. Baptism Signifies Death and Resurrection

Baptism, then, signifies two things—death and resurrection, that is, full and complete justification. . . . When the minister immerses the child in the water it signifies death, and when he draws it forth again it signifies life [Romans 6:4]. . . . This death and resurrection we call the new creation, regeneration, and spiritual birth. . . . As long as we are in the flesh, the desires of the flesh stir and are stirred. For this reason, as soon as we begin to believe, we also begin to die to this world and live to God in the life to come; so that faith is truly a death and a resurrection, that is, it is that spiritual baptism into which we are submerged and from which we rise. (*LW* 36:67–68)

For Luther, baptism is the sacrament signifying death and resurrection. It is death to the condemning power of sin; and rising to new life as God's children of grace and justified persons.

Our resurrection is variously named: new creation, regeneration, and spiritual birth. It is the most important thing that can happen to a person. It is justification by faith in a distinctly visible form.

Baptism does not exempt Christians from the ongoing power of sin. Christians sin. But baptism is God's promise and the mark that these sins do not doom us. In baptism, we begin to live as persons who are "at the same time righteous and a sinner" (see #25). In our new life we struggle as we die to sin and "live to God in the life to come." In baptism, we have God's pledge and covenant that our sins are not "a cause for condemnation." In our new life we can "call upon God's mercy" (*LW* 35:35).

Living as a Christian

36. Christian Life as Daily Baptism

> These two parts, being dipped under the water and emerging from it, point to the power and effect of baptism, which is nothing else than the slaying of the old Adam and the resurrection of the new creature, both of which must continue in us our whole life long. Thus a Christian life is nothing else than a daily baptism, begun once and continuing ever after.[5]

Baptism is at the center of Christian life for Luther. It marks a person's new identity because here there is "the slaying of the old Adam and the resurrection of the new creature." This movement is from death to new life.

Baptism is central because its effects "must continue in us our whole life long." Luther said baptism is "not a matter of the moment, but something permanent. Although the ceremony itself is soon over the thing it signifies continues until we die, yes, even until we rise on the last day" (*LW* 36:69). Baptism lasts.

In short, "a Christian life is nothing else than a daily baptism, begun once and continuing ever after."[6] In faith we hold fast to baptism, finding it to be "the ground of all comfort," knowing that even when we sin, God "will not count my sin against me" (*LW* 35:36). As we struggle with temptation and sin, we remember our baptism and trust God's ongoing presence and power—expressed in baptism—to be ours, through all the steps of our Christian lives.

As we die to sin daily, let us remember our baptism!

37. Faces of the Lord

In the Old Testament faces of the Lord were the pillar
of fire, the cloud, and the mercy seat; in the New Testament, Baptism, the Lord's Supper, the ministry of the
Word, and the like. By means of these God shows us, as
by a visible sign, that He is with us, takes care of us, and
is favorably inclined toward us. (*LW* 1:309)

On our journey through the Christian life, we need continual
ways of experiencing God's presence and help. God has pro-
vided these in full measure!

Luther notes the way the people of Israel in the Old Testament experienced the "faces of the Lord" as they traveled
through the wilderness toward the promised land. Through the
pillar of cloud by day and the pillar of fire by night, God led
the people (Exod. 13:17–22). Traveling on, they experienced
the presence of God in the mercy seat covering the ark of the
covenant (Exod. 25:10–22). Here the people met God (25:22).

In the New Testament, the faces of the Lord are in "Baptism, the Lord's Supper, the ministry of the Word, and the like."
These are visible signs through which God shows us that God
is always with us, takes care of us, and is "favorably inclined
toward us."

These are resources we need as we seek to be the people of
God in the church who are disciples of Jesus Christ. God works
through outward, visible signs to strengthen our faith and give
us the assurances we need as we live out our faith. The church
is where these faces of the Lord are experienced. Thank God for
giving us these ways to help us. As we participate in the church's
ongoing life, we are blessed with God's face shining on us.

38. Everything Is a Gift of God

Scripture directs us to this humility so that we may not become proud because of our gifts but may maintain that they are not ours but God's; then we shall praise God with one accord and give thanks to him. . . . Everything we have is ours solely as a favor and gift of God. (*LW* 2:392, 393)

Sometimes it is easy to believe all we have and have achieved has come because of our own abilities and wisdom. We hear of "self-made persons," those who have prospered because of efforts that have brought what they wanted, even "the finer things of life."

But attitudes of self-sufficiency go counter to Scripture. Luther points out that humility should be our posture when we receive gifts. We should not become "proud"—an attitude that Scripture roundly condemns when it comes to recognizing the source of what we have been given. Humility maintains that the gifts we receive "are not ours but God's." Our proper response is to praise God, as the people of Israel did when they recognized God acted on behalf of the nation.

The bottom line is that "everything we have is ours solely as a favor and gift of God." This puts things in proper perspective. God's favor and gifts are given in the totality of our lives, as "everything we have." The source of all blessings, whatever forms they take—is God. No "self-sufficiency" here; no sense of "achievement" that glorifies the works of our hands, as the works of our hands.

We praise God and give thanks to God because we know our blessings come from the Lord. God's favor and gifts are the most wonderful blessings we can receive. In humility, we accept God's graciousness to us, in gratitude. All is from God!

39. Treasure
beyond Temporal Goods

The temporal goods you have, God has given to you for this life. He does permit you to use them and with them to fill the bag of worms that you wear around your neck. But you should not fasten or hang your heart on them as though you were going to live forever. You should always go on and consider another, higher, and better treasure, which is your own and which will last forever. (*LW* 21:13)

A teaching Jesus gave in his Sermon on the Mount was: "Blessed are the poor in spirit, for theirs is the kingdom of heaven" (Matt. 5:3). Christians have wondered whether Matthew's account means Christians must be in physical poverty as well as being "poor in spirit."

Luther believed "having money, property, land, and retinue outwardly is not wrong in itself. It is God's gift and ordinance" (*LW* 21:12). He pointed out that "the world could not endure if we were all to be beggars and to have nothing" (*LW* 21:12).

God does give "temporal goods" for "this life." But we should "use all temporal goods and physical necessities, the way a guest does in a strange place." Our possessions are temporary and do not belong to us "by right." Most important is that "you should not fasten or hang your heart on them as though you were going to live forever." We must not set our "confidence, comfort, and trust on temporal goods," so they become idols to us.

Before God, "everyone must be spiritually poor." We are to look for "another, higher, and better treasure, which is your own and which will last forever."

40. Lifelong Repentance

When our Lord and Master Jesus Christ said, "Repent" [Matt. 4:17], he willed the entire life of believers to be one of repentance. (*LW* 31:25)

The first of Luther's Ninety-five Theses conveyed his vision of the Christian life as marked by continual repentance. The "entire life of believers" features repentance as an ongoing practice. This Luther drew from Jesus' proclamation at the beginning of his ministry: "Repent, for the kingdom of heaven has come near" (Matt. 4:17).

In explaining his thesis, Luther wrote about this verse and its implications: "We pray throughout our whole life and we must pray 'forgive us our debts' [Matthew 6:12]; therefore, we repent throughout our whole life and are displeased with ourselves, unless anyone may be so foolish as to think he must only pretend to pray for the forgiveness of debts" (*LW* 31:84–85). In the Lord's Prayer, Jesus recognized his disciples will continually need forgiveness for their sins, so he prescribed that they pray, "Forgive us our debts."

Theologically, Christian believers see in the law of God that they sin. Christians struggle against sin. Believers, said Luther, are "at the same time righteous and a sinner" (see #25). We are justified by faith and are accounted righteous before God on the basis of the work of Jesus Christ. Our sin is forgiven on the basis of the work of Christ. But we still sin.

Yet now, when believers sin, God's Spirit leads us to repent and seek forgiveness. Sin is serious for Christ's disciples. We all have to examine our lives and realize the ways we break God's law and fall short of God's will for us. So we pray; and so we repent — our whole life long.

41. Turning from Our Evil Ways

"To turn from one's evil way" is not a trivial work; it does not involve fasting and wearing sackcloth, but believing in God with all one's heart and loving the neighbor as one's self; that is, it demands piety and righteousness in one's whole being, both inwardly and outwardly, in body and soul. God wants the entire person. He has an aversion to shilly-shallying and hypocritical people. (*LW* 19:90)

Luther saw the story of the prophet Jonah, who preached to the people of Nineveh that they should turn from their evil ways or else face destruction, as showing what true turning away from evil and turning to God should mean.

The people responded to Jonah's preaching and "believed God." They proclaimed a fast and put on sackcloth (Jonah 3:5). But this is not what it rightly means to turn from evil ways. Instead, says Luther, turning from evil — repentance — means "believing in God with all one's heart and loving one's neighbor as one's self." Here Luther echoed Jesus' summary of the law of God: love God and love your neighbor (Mark 12:30–31). Inner belief and total love to God and neighbor is needed for outward actions to have meaning. God desires there be "piety and righteousness in one's whole being, both inwardly and outwardly, in body and soul."

Luther put it simply, but with penetrating seriousness: "God wants the entire person." No parts of our lives, no agendas, attitudes, or actions, no desires, can remain outside our love for God or excuses for not loving neighbors in meaningful ways. Everything we are expresses our love for God and neighbor. For God has "an aversion to shilly-shallying and hypocritical people." Only love of God and neighbor shows true turning from our evil ways.

42. Free and a Servant of All

A Christian is a perfectly free lord of all, subject to none.
A Christian is a perfectly dutiful servant of all, subject
to all. (*LW* 31:344)

In Luther's important work, *The Freedom of a Christian* (1520),
he discussed the Christian's relationship with God and to the
world. In his "Open Letter to Pope Leo X," Luther said this
treatise "contains the whole of Christian life in a brief form"
(*LW* 31:343).

Luther defended two propositions: "A Christian is lord of
all, completely free of everything; a Christian is servant of all,
completely attentive to the needs of all."[7] These dialectical and
paradoxical sentences captured Luther's view of "the whole of
Christian life."

Christians are free from sin through faith in Jesus Christ.
We are justified by faith and not works. We do not try to gain
salvation by obeying the law of God, which we are unable to
do. We receive salvation by God's grace through faith in Jesus
Christ. So Christians are "lord of all, completely free of everything"—free from trying to justify themselves before God.

But in relation to the world and neighbors, a Christian is
"servant of all, completely attentive to the needs of all." We are
bound to serve our neighbors by love. We are obliged to serve
them, even as Jesus Christ loved and served us (John 15:12).
In faith we are free to serve others in love. Our freedom is to do
good works. These demonstrate faith. They are compassionate,
loving care of neighbors.

43. The Christian's Clothing: Faith and Love

The clothing of Christians is twofold—faith and love—
just as Christ had on two coats: one undivided, which
signifies faith, and the other divided, which signifies
love [John 19:23–24]. (*LW* 76:289)

Luther uses a scene from the crucifixion of Jesus to speak figu-
ratively of "the clothing of Christians." John's Gospel indicates
Jesus' clothes were divided among the soldiers, but his tunic,
which was seamless, was not divided. It went to the soldier who
won the lot cast for it (John 19:23–24).

Luther interprets Christ's "two coats" to be "one undivided,
which signifies faith, and the other divided, which signifies
love." These, he says are the "clothing of Christians."

In theological detail, Luther wrote of "what an entire Christian life should be, namely, faith and love: faith in God, which
apprehends Christ and receives forgiveness of sins apart from
all works, and after that love toward the neighbor, which as the
fruit of faith proves that faith is true and not lazy or false, but
active and living" (*LW* 38:184).

What we believe and what we do make up the life of the
Christian. Our faith proclaims God in Christ and provides "forgiveness of sins apart from all works"—by God's sheer grace.
Our faith propels us to "love toward neighbor." This is the "fruit
of faith," its right expression, for which we have been set free
by God's grace. Our love toward neighbors shows the truth of
our faith—that it comes from God in Christ; and it is "not lazy
or false, but active and living." As the old expression puts it,
"we are not saved to sit; we are saved to serve." We wear our
clothing!

44. Eyes of Faith

> This star is the bodily preaching and the bright revelation of Christ as He was concealed and promised in Scripture. . . . It is impossible for Christ and His Gospel to be recognized by reason; only faith recognizes them. And "seeing the star" signifies this faith. (*LW* 76:112, 113)

Luther often contrasts human reason with faith. While reason has its place, it is not our guide in matters of faith. For Luther, "faith tells you what you cannot judge and settle with your reason. Faith closes the eyes of reason. . . . We must not brew together faith and reason. . . . We must abandon reason and listen to God's Word alone" (*LW* 68:24, 26).

Faith is seeing things that are not apparent or visible by human perceptions. Faith is, says Luther, "an understanding in concealment because it deals with those things which a man cannot know of himself" (*LW* 25:224). As God is concealed in the cross of Christ (see #6), so faith sees God who is concealed in things that can seem contrary to God.

The magi followed the star at the birth of Jesus. To others, it would appear as only a "star." To the eyes of faith, it was "the bright revelation of Christ as He was concealed and promised in Scripture." Luther maintains "it is impossible for Christ and His Gospel to be recognized by reason; only faith recognizes them. And 'seeing the star' signifies this faith."

For Luther, sometimes God is actually hidden. This is real. Other times, faith sees God in the midst of situations and circumstances where it can appear that God is absent.

45. Daring Confidence in God's Grace

Faith is a living, daring confidence in God's grace, so sure and certain that the believer would stake his life on it a thousand times. This knowledge of and confidence in God's grace makes men glad and bold and happy in dealing with God and with all creatures. And this is the work which the Holy Spirit performs in faith. (*LW* 35:370)

We use the word "faith" in different ways. We speak of having "faith" in our doctors, in our sports teams, even having "faith" in the brakes of our car. In different realms of life, we refer to "faith."

Christian faith focuses on God and what God has done in Jesus Christ. God's grace or free favor is expressed in Christ. We are justified or saved by God's grace in Jesus Christ, which we receive by faith, or trust. We live by faith. We live as those who know God's grace in Christ.

This faith, says Luther, is "a living, daring confidence in God's grace, so sure and certain that the believer would stake his life on it a thousand times." It is an active faith, working through love. It is faith that propels us into serving God through serving neighbors and which can lead us through all situations in life. We stake our lives on God's grace, trusting that God is "sure and certain."

Living in faith this way gives us confidence and makes us glad and happy. The Holy Spirit brings this gift of faith to us and enables us to live this way. "Daring confidence in God's grace" enables us to live in freedom, the freedom to love and serve God and meet human need. God's Spirit is with us. We are glad, bold, and happy!

46. Faith Active through Love

This is a truly Christian life. Here faith is truly active through love [Gal. 5:6], that is, it finds expression in works of the freest service, cheerfully and lovingly done, with which a man willingly serves another without hope of reward; and for himself he is satisfied with the fullness and wealth of his faith. (*LW* 31:365)

The Christian is a free person, free before God in Jesus Christ; and free to serve others through love. "This is," says Luther, "a truly Christian life."

The "faith alone" that justifies us in Jesus Christ is not a faith that is "alone," never expressing itself. Faith as "a daring confidence in God's grace" (see #45), as Luther expressed it, is free to serve others in acts of compassion, justice, and peace. The needs of others will become foremost in the hearts of disciples of Jesus Christ. The church is the context where others can be served. But Christians serve their neighbors wherever they are found or whatever needs emerge.

These works "of the freest service" are "cheerfully and lovingly done." Our service to others rises from faith in Christ, which imitates our Master. Love is given "without hope of reward." Our good works do not save us nor are they a focus for Christians. Faith active through love is willingly and joyfully rendered, because faith itself provides a "fullness and wealth" that nothing else can match and that emerges from the depth of faith itself.

No wonder this is "truly a Christian life"! Luther knew, as Paul said, "The only thing that counts is faith working through love" (Gal. 5:6). Works freely done through love of others are the fullest and most wonderful expression of faith!

47. Upholding the Suffering and Sorrow of Others

You must in turn share the misfortunes of the fellowship. . . . Every bane and blessing of all the saints on earth affects them [the saints]. Here your heart must go out in love and learn that this is a sacrament of love. As love and support are given you, you in turn must render love and support to Christ in his needy ones. . . . You must feel with sorrow . . . all the unjust suffering of the innocent, with which the world is everywhere filled to overflowing. . . . As you uphold all of them, so they all in turn uphold you; and all things are in common, both good and evil. (*LW* 35:54)

Our unity with Christ and each other in the church commits us to radical care for the needs of others. We "share the misfortunes of the fellowship" so that "every bane and blessing of all the saints on earth" affects us. This is to take on a wide world of concern, since our heart "must go out in love."

For Luther, the sacrament of the Lord's Supper is "a sacrament of love." It puts before us the deep love of God in Jesus Christ and commits us to this deep love for others. "As love and support are given you," said Luther, "you in turn must render love and support to Christ in his needy ones." This is not an option. It is the directions our hearts move when we participate in the sacrament of love.

Our commitment means that "you must feel with sorrow . . . all the unjust suffering of the innocent, with which the world is everywhere filled to overflowing." Innocent suffering, injustices, meeting needs—all "good and evil" is shared with others. For "as you uphold all of them, so they all in turn uphold you." This is the church.

48. Mighty Bones to Bear Burdens

To love does not mean, as the sophists imagine, to wish someone else well, but to bear someone else's burdens, that is, to bear what is burdensome to you and what you would rather not bear. Therefore a Christian must have broad shoulders and husky bones to carry the flesh, that is, the weakness, of the brethren; for Paul says that they have burdens and troubles. . . . Let us bear those of others . . . in accordance with the statements: "Bear one another's burdens" and "You shall love your neighbor as yourself" (Lev. 19:18). (*LW* 27:113)

Here, Luther speaks about the meaning of love as not simply "well-wishing" but as "burden-bearing." From the Old Testament commandment to love our neighbor (Lev. 19:18) and Paul's injunction: "Bear one another's burdens, and in this way you will fulfill the law of Christ" (Gal. 6:2), we see how faith can be active in love (Gal. 5:6).

Luther's image for the Christian as burden-bearer is memorable. In a sixteenth-century English translation, the picturesque phrase was "Christians must have strong shoulders and mighty bones." The current translation says, "broad shoulders and husky bones." These are needed to carry the "flesh, that is, the weakness" of sisters and brothers. Indeed, says Luther, Paul knew—as we do—that others have "burdens and troubles." The center of Christian life in the church is to bear these burdens.

Burden-bearing takes many forms for us. Luther went on to mention "faults and sins" as burdens to be carried—and shared. We can think of so many more burdens. Whatever afflicts others is embraced in the ministry of burden-bearing. We bear because we care. Others share their burdens with us; as we do with them. This fulfills the law of Christ, the law of love.

49. The Supper and a Community of Love

O this is a great sacrament, says St. Paul, that Christ and the church are one flesh and bone. Again through this same love, we are to be changed and to make the infirmities of all other Christians our own; we are to take upon ourselves their form and their necessity, and all the good that is within our power we are to make theirs, that they may profit from it. That is real fellowship, and that is the true significance of this sacrament. In this way we are changed into one another and are made into a community by love. Without love there can be no such change. (*LW* 35:58)

Our love and service to others is grounded in God's love in Jesus Christ, who came among us as "one who serves" (Luke 22:27).

This love is visible in the sacrament of the Lord's Supper. In giving himself for sin through his death on the cross, Jesus expressed the deepest and most important love we know. This is what is celebrated in the Supper: "This is my body" and "This is my blood" (Luke 22:19, 20).

The love that unites Christ with the church as "one flesh and bone," changes us into those who "make the infirmities of all other Christians our own." We reach out in love to take on the needs and difficulties of others. Also, "all the good that is within our power we are to make theirs." We share ourselves and our resources to enhance the lives of others.

This is "the true significance of the sacrament," says Luther. The church is a fellowship, a community of love where "we are changed into one another." Christ's love does it. For "without love there can be no such change."

50. Living in Christ and Neighbor

We conclude, therefore, that a Christian lives not in himself, but in Christ and in his neighbor. Otherwise he is not a Christian. He lives in Christ through faith, in his neighbor through love. By faith he is caught up beyond himself into God. By love he descends beneath himself into his neighbor. Yet he always remains in God and in his love. (*LW* 31:371)

Our primary identity in Christian faith is that believers are "in Christ." We are united with Jesus Christ by faith (Rom. 8:1). Our lives are "hidden with Christ in God" (Col. 3:3). So we do not live in ourselves. Now, it is "Christ who lives in me. And the life I now live in the flesh I live by faith in the Son of God, who loved me and gave himself for me" (Gal. 2:20).

Luther focuses on this identity in Christ when he says Christians live, not in ourselves, but in Christ and in our neighbors. Otherwise, we are "not a Christian." Without this sense of life in Christ and life in our neighbor, we are apart from Christ.

We live in Christ by faith; and in our neighbor "through love." Luther continually refers to this twofold existence — that our faith must show itself in love toward others. The movement is "upward" to God in faith and "outward" to neighbors in love. These are the two directions in which we live as those who are "in Christ." Do we live in these ways?

Difficult as it can be to maintain our faith or to love our neighbor — who may seem totally unlovable at times — we must keep our focus. This can happen because we know that we always remain "in God" and in God's love. Nothing could be better!

51. To Love Your Neighbor

To love your neighbor as yourself means to love in such a way that you set aside knowledge, property, and honor, and instead seek your neighbor's benefit and well-being and set it before your own benefit. (*LW* 68:44)

Jesus emphasized the need to "love your neighbor as yourself" when he named this law of God (Lev. 19:18) along with loving God with all that is within us as the greatest commandments (Matt. 22:34–40).

Luther's description of what it means to love your neighbor is far-reaching. It asks us to "set aside knowledge, property, and honor, and instead seek your neighbor's benefit and well-being and set it before your own benefit." This is a comprehensive prescription, more of which could not be asked.

Given the sinfulness of the human condition, Luther knew this was not an easy command of Jesus to follow. The experience of faith, which frees us from sin's power to bind us to ourselves, is broken by Christ. Now believers are a "new creation" (2 Cor. 5:17) who desire to love and serve Christ by serving others. Luther said that this means we recognize "the good things we have from God should flow from one to the other and be common to all" (*LW* 31:371). We seek the "benefit and well-being" of others, sharing with them, before we promote ourselves. This is a true conversion: from me to neighbor.

Some persons of faith sacrifice themselves dramatically for others. Yet there are daily opportunities for us to love others in ordinary but significant ways. Will we give our time, our resources, and our care to our neighbors to share the love of Christ?

52. Be the Servant to Your Neighbor

> It has often and abundantly been said enough in other postils that we also are to lay aside our glorious form and serve others. God wants each one to be the servant of his neighbor with body, property, honor, spirit, and soul, just as His Son has done for us. (*LW* 76:423)

In a Palm Sunday sermon, Luther preached on Philippians 2:5–11. This great passage speaks of Jesus Christ, "who, though he was in the form of God . . . emptied himself, taking the form of a slave . . . and became obedient to the point of death—even death on a cross." Luther said this passage "presents us with the powerful example of . . . the love of Christ—in order to incite us to practice love for one another." Paul, noted Luther, "certainly has seen how lax and lazy Christians are in love" (*LW* 76:415).

This Philippian passage is an important description of how Jesus Christ, who existed eternally in the "form of God," came to earth, humbled himself, becoming a servant (slave), and dying for human sin. Theologically, this is Jesus' "humiliation," his giving up his heavenly "form" to become a "servant" for us.

Luther concluded his sermon by indicating that Christ is the model for us in serving others: "We also are to lay aside our glorious form and serve others. God wants each one to be the servant of his neighbor with body, property, honor, spirit, and soul, just as His Son has done for us." The fullness of Christ's giving himself for us—even suffering death on the cross—stands before us. Now Christ enables us to "lay aside our glorious form" and to "serve others"—if only we will!

53. Look for the Angels in Your Neighbor

The angels like nothing more than to watch us deal with the Word of God; with such people they enjoy dwelling. Therefore leave the angels up there in heaven undisturbed. Look for them here on earth below, in your neighbor, father and mother, children, and others. Do for these what God has commanded, and the angels will never be far away from you. (*LW* 21:36)

In commenting on Jesus' words: "Blessed are the pure in heart, for they will see God" (Matt. 5:8), Luther discussed those who, because of their religious devotion, do not want to have anything to do with other people. They believe their inward purity is defiled by associations with others: "They think that they alone are pure and that other people are impure." They think that being of help or serving their neighbor means they would "be committing a most grievous sin and defiling themselves altogether" (*LW* 21:35). One religious hermit believed "the angels cannot come to anyone who moves around in human society."

Though we may not know people with these extreme views, the stories warn us about isolating ourselves and neglecting others. Luther further said that one can leave the angels "up there in heaven." The right place to look for angels is "here on earth below, in your neighbor, father and mother, children, and others." This is what God has commanded (cf. Exod. 20:12). If we "do for these what God has commanded," then "the angels will never be far away from you." We see God's angels in the persons God gives us to love and serve. Look for the angels in others!

54. Don't Be a Skinflint

> To become a skinflint and treasure the penny so highly
> that you do not even permit yourself and others to use it,
> and even forget about God and your neighbor contrary
> to the First Commandment, that is truly a base vice, and
> the devil prompts the people to do this. (*LW* 68:54)

A "skinflint" is a miser, one who will spend as little money as possible. This is a derogatory term, but sometimes may not be taken too seriously.

Luther saw the "skinflint" as dangerous. He denounced those who "treasure the penny so highly" that they will not share wealth while they "forget about God" and neighbor along the way. This attitude is a special danger for the rich; but it can infect anyone.

This is so perilous because it makes an idol out of what we have. We trust riches, making them into our "god" so that they become idols. This violates the First Commandment (Exod. 20:4), as Luther said. The "penny" becomes an idol.

The effect is that our wealth, which is "God's gift," is not used in a "Christian manner" and one forgets about God and neighbor (*LW* 68:53). A person like this, Luther scathingly says, "cannot be saved." For that person is "without God and has no part of God's kingdom. Someone like that expels God from his heart and puts mammon [wealth] in His place." "In Wealth We Trust" becomes a motto.

Miserly idolatry chokes our responsibilities to God and neighbors. To catch what Jesus means: "You cannot serve God and cash" (Matt. 6:24).

55. Seize Every Opportunity to Help Our Neighbor

Then let us show mercy to our neighbor, that is, let it be our pleasure to help a neighbor, to seize every opportunity to help a neighbor. Let us also stir up others to perform the responsibilities of love, so that in this way our entire life yields to the good of our neighbor, since we owe nothing to anyone, except that we love him, Rom. 13:8. (*LW* 18:261)

Luther's phrase, "show mercy" comes from his interpreting Micah 6:8, one of the great texts of the Old Testament. A phrase here is that God requires us to "show mercy" or "love mercy." Luther says, "This means that it pleases us to be blessings to others, for the Hebrew word (חֶסֶד) [*ḥesed*] properly means mercy that has been shown, as Christ also indicates in Matthew 9:13: "Go and learn what this means, 'I desire mercy and not sacrifice.'"

God requires us to love and show mercy and bless others — just as God in Jesus Christ — has shown mercy to us. Luther notes, we are not justified by works — presenting "sacrifices." We are justified by faith, to which we should witness in proclaiming God's grace.

We do this is by showing mercy to our neighbor, letting it be "our pleasure to help a neighbor." This is our joy. Luther says we should "seize every opportunity to help a neighbor." We are on the lookout for ways to help, even as we also "stir up others to perform the responsibilities of love." We should "share care," so to speak — take initiatives with others who can show care and love for others. This can surely be extended societally, as well. We live so that "our entire life yields to the good of our neighbor." May we!

56. Do Good When Enemies Need It

> Look at how high He puts the target. Not only does He denounce those who do harm to their enemies, but He also refuses to call those "pious" who neglect to do them good when they need it. He says first: "Love your enemies." But "to love" means to be goodhearted and to wish the best, to have a heart that is friendly, kind, and sweet toward everyone, not one that makes fun of misery or misfortune. (*LW* 21:122)

Jesus' command: "Love your enemies" (Matt. 5:44) is sometimes called the hardest command of all. Imagine—loving your adversaries, foes, rivals, competitors! This runs counter to our inclinations and culture practices.

Luther says that "the commandment (Leviticus 19:18): 'You shall love your neighbor as yourself,' applies to the common crowd and to each individual in particular." Jesus sets a "high target" here.

Luther interpreted Jesus as denouncing "those who do harm to their enemies." These are their outright actions against others. But, there are sins of omission here, too. Jesus "refuses to call those 'pious' who neglect to do them good when they need it." This is what makes the command so difficult. Why not do nothing to help enemies, when they are in need? Ignoring and overlooking opportunities to serve enemies, that's the natural reaction—perhaps even for Christians.

But "to love," said Luther, means "to be goodhearted and to wish the best, to have a heart that is friendly, kind, and sweet toward everyone"—even to enemies! These are attitudes of love and should be ours. They are to orient the lives of Jesus' disciples. Yet active love will also go further (cf. Luke 6:27–36). It will seek to serve—even enemies. Will we follow Jesus' command?

57. Faith from the Heart's Core

"Thou shalt have no other gods." This means, "Since I alone am God, thou shalt place all thy confidence, trust, and faith in me alone and in no one else." . . . And this faith, this trust, this confidence from the heart's core is the true fulfilling of the first commandment. Without such faith no work at all can satisfy this command. (*LW* 44:30)

The first of the Ten Commandments: "Thou shalt have no other gods," is interpreted by Luther to mean God says, that "since I alone am God, thou shalt place all thy confidence, trust, and faith in me alone and in no one else." This is a comprehensive demand! But it is the basic orientation of our lives of faith.

We are tempted to turn away from this singular focus. We are lured into idolatry—having other "gods" to worship or in which to put our trust. We trust our own abilities, what we can do or what we want—instead of putting all our confidence, trust, and faith in God alone and "no one else."

To navigate our temptations and afflictions, we need to be centered on God alone. We need faith that comes "from the heart's core," says Luther. This is "the true fulfilling of the first commandment." Our heart's core expresses faith in the one true and living God. Without this faith, "no work at all can satisfy this command." All the other commandments of God are contained in this First Commandment. Faith is God's real intention in this commandment. This commandment demands trust in God alone, "from the heart's core." Faith is this trust. Our heart and trust acknowledge God as the source of all good; and no "other gods" are to be worshiped.

How is your heart's core?

58. Lead Us Not into Temptation

In the *Lives of the Fathers* we find another illustration. There someone says that these thoughts are like birds that fly about in the open sky. It does not, so he says, lie within our power to stop them from flying about over our heads. But it does lie within our power to stop them from building nests in our hair. (*LW* 13:113)

Temptation to sin is an ongoing part of our Christian lives. Every day, temptations come to us. No matter how we try to escape encountering them, temptations arise. This is a reality for all Christians.

In discussing temptation, Luther referred to the *Lives of the Fathers*, stories about lives of figures from the early church. He mentions an illustration about the thoughts that lead to temptation being "like birds that fly about in the open sky." We cannot stop the birds "from flying about over our heads." But, "it does lie within our power to stop them from building nests in our hair."

The meaning of it, said Luther, is that "such thoughts originate in a cause outside us: in the devil. We cannot prevent them from coming toward us. But we can be on our guard when they arrive, and we need not embrace them and thus be led away into sin" (*LW* 13:114).

We cannot avoid temptations approaching to us. But we can resist them and prevent them from taking root in our lives or leading us away from God's will and purposes.

Luther's comments imply that when dealing with temptation, to watch the first step. When tempted, at the very beginning, we need to be "on our guard." We must close the door against and give no opportunity for the birds to build their nests in our hair!

59. Run to the Lord's Prayer

When you feel such temptations, go running to the
Lord's Prayer! You have the promise that God will
deliver you from the temptation of the flesh, the world,
and the devil. Our whole life is nothing but temptation
by these three, the flesh, the world, the devil. Therefore pray: Father, let not our flesh seduce us, let not the
world deceive us, let not the devil cast us down. (*LW*
51:180)

Temptations of many sorts daily present themselves to us. Some
are harder to resist than others. But being tempted: to turn from
God's way to the way we want or to disregard God's Word to
trust ourselves and cater to our own wishes—these experiences
are very real.

We need help to resist temptation and faithfully follow of
our Master, Jesus Christ. When we feel tempted, Luther urges,
"go running to the Lord's Prayer!" The major sources of our
difficulties—"the temptation of the flesh, the world, and the
devil"—can be overcome. We deal with these, always. Says
Luther, "our whole life is nothing but temptation by these three,
the flesh, the world, the devil."

But whatever the source of our temptations or how they
come to us, the help is to "go running to the Lord's Prayer!" The
prayer Jesus taught his disciples focuses on where our minds
and hearts should be. We pray, "lead us not into temptation, but
deliver us from evil" (or, "do not bring us to the time of trial, but
rescue us from the evil one" [Matt. 6:13]). Luther says: "Pray:
Father, let not our flesh seduce us, let not the world deceive us,
let not the devil cast us down."

When tempted, run to the Lord's Prayer!

60. Yielding to the Divine Will

He should by no means insist on deliverance from these trials without yielding to the divine will. He should address God cheerfully and firmly and say, "If I am to drink this cup, dear Father, may your will, not mine, be done" [Luke 22:42]. (*LW* 42:183)

Throughout his life as a theologian, Luther was beset by the affliction of *Anfechtung*. This German term represented a testing of his faith by an assault on his whole self. The term cannot be captured fully in English. But for Luther it involved fear, his burdened conscience, his recognition of sin, and a sense of guilt. It may come as an attack of the devil or from the "hidden God," whose absence is a test of faith. Doubt, despair, and desperation resulted.

Luther's 1521 treatise, *Comfort When Facing Grave Temptations*, lists some ways to deal with "temptations" (*Anfechtung* is in the German text). His most basic advice was that in these trials and afflictions, one must yield to the divine will. Alluding to Jesus' prayer in the Garden of Gethsemane on the eve of his death, when Jesus prayed, "Not my will but yours be done," Luther said one should "address God cheerfully and firmly and say, 'If I am to drink this cup, dear Father, may your will, not mine, be done'" (Luke 22:42).

This is the ultimate recourse in affliction and temptation. Faith means that in the face of overwhelming difficulties, we turn situations over to God, trust in God, and ask that not our will but God's will be done. This is naked faith and pure trust. Jesus' affliction led him to the cross; but it also led him to resurrection.

In all our struggles, faith is the opposite of *Anfechtung*. In trust, we yield to the divine will.

61. Rejoice Most When Things Are Worst

Christians are adapted so that they have no joy in temporal abundance and comfort, but only in God. For that reason they rejoice the most when things are going the worst according to the flesh. The further they turn away from temporal treasures, the closer God is to them with His future treasures. So St. Paul lists joy among the fruits of the Spirit (Galatians 5[:22]), since the flesh does not produce such joy. Elsewhere he speaks of "joy in the Holy Spirit" (Romans 14[:17]). (*LW* 76:225)

Our only comfort is in God.

It is easy to lose sight of this. "The godless," says Luther, "rejoice when they have sufficient property, honor, and comfort, but are sad when the weather changes." For "their joy is an untimely joy, and their sadness is an untimely sadness, for they rejoice when it is a time of sadness, and they are sad when it is a time of joy" (*LW* 76:224–25). They focus on themselves instead of God.

Joy for Christians focuses not on "the world" but on God who urges us: "Rejoice in hope, be patient in suffering, persevere in prayer" (Rom. 12:12). This turns the Christian's attention where it ought to be; not in "temporal abundance and comfort, but only in God."

It seems counterintuitive, but Christians "rejoice the most when things are going the worst according to the flesh." Christians turn away from "temporal treasures" when God is close "to them with His future treasures." We have future treasures. This is our true joy, even when things are at their worst!

62. Think of Christ in Suffering and Affliction

> When the suffering and affliction is at its worst, it bears and presses down so grievously that one thinks he can endure no more and must surely perish. But then if you can think of Christ, the faithful God will come and will help you, as he has always helped his own from the beginning of the world; for he is the same God as he always has been. (*LW* 51:200)

Sometimes we think we just cannot make it any further. Suffering and affliction "bears and presses down so grievously," says Luther, "that one thinks he can endure no more and must surely perish." We know what this feels like. We are at the end of our rope. We cannot help ourselves or do anything to remedy our situation.

What to do?

Luther says in the midst of our most grievous situations, if we can "think of Christ, the faithful God will come and will help you, as he has always helped his own from the beginning of the world; for he is the same God as he always has been." When we think of Christ, we see God's faithfulness in the person of the Son of God. God sent Jesus Christ into the world "to save sinners" (1 Timothy 1:15). Christ came to help us. God is the same God who, through the Old and New Testaments, comes to help God's people. Thinking of Christ means we know God will help us. We think of Luther's hymn, *A Mighty Fortress Is Our God*, and the line, "Our helper He amid the flood." God is our help through every and all the "floods" of suffering and affliction with which we have to deal.

Think of Christ, always!

63. Promises in Sufferings

We have so many assurances and promises that he will not allow us to stick in our suffering but will help us out of it, even though all men should doubt it. Therefore, even though it hurts, so be it, you have to go through some suffering anyhow; things cannot always go smoothly. It is just as well, nay, a thousand times better, to have suffered for the sake of Christ, who promised us comfort and help in suffering, than to suffer and despair and perish without comfort and help for the sake of the devil. (*LW* 51:208)

Suffering is part of the Christian life. Christ's disciples "deny themselves and take up their cross and follow me" (Mark 8:34). Taking up our cross leads to sufferings for the sake of Christ since we are following Jesus' way in a hostile world. Our sufferings can take many forms and vary throughout our lives. Though we willingly suffer for the sake of Christ, the suffering is still real and painful.

Yet Luther affirms, "we have so many assurances and promises" that God will not allow us to "stick in our suffering but will help us out of it, even though all men should doubt it." No matter how impossible things look or how heavy our burdens, God promises to help us through our sufferings. We have no greater blessing than this!

"Things cannot always go smoothly," said Luther. But the promises of God's help through our sufferings assure us that we will not be stuck in them forever and that God will help us out of it. When we suffer for the sake of Christ, this is our comfort and hope. We trust God to see us through!

64. Forgiveness of Sins — The Sum of the Gospel

> If I preach the forgiveness of sins, I preach the true Gospel. The sum of the Gospel is this: whoever believes in Christ has his sins forgiven. . . . The Gospel should unceasingly sound and ring in the mouth of all Christians. (*LW* 76:436)

Luther's great discovery of the doctrine of justification by faith means that by God's grace, human sin is forgiven on the basis of the death and resurrection of Jesus Christ. This, for Luther, was the "sum of the Gospel."

Christian preachers can preach "absolution," said Luther. Sin is forgiven and peace is given, just as Jesus announced to his disciples after his resurrection: "*Pax vobis*, 'Peace be with you' [John 20:19, 21, 26]." The sacrament of the Lord's Supper does this too: "'This is My body which is given for you; this is My blood which is poured out for you for the forgiveness of sins,' etc. [cf. Matt. 26:26–28]." This promise means, says Luther, that "whoever believes in Christ has his sins forgiven." Even if some sins are forgotten, "they are still forgiven, for God does not look at how well you confess but at His Word and how you believe it" (*LW* 76:439). If God is "gracious to you, then all sins must be gone." We can "always rely on God's Word against sin and an evil conscience" (*LW* 76:439).

No wonder Luther proclaimed that "the Gospel should unceasingly sound and ring in the mouth of all Christians." The true gospel is the greatest news we can ever hear; and it is the greatest message we can ever proclaim! Our deepest problem — sin — is met by the forgiveness God gives in Jesus Christ. Praise!

65. Forgive One Another in Every Situation

The doctrine of the forgiveness of sins is the most important of all, both for us personally and for our relations with others. As Christ continually bears with us in His kingdom and forgives us all sorts of faults, so we should bear and forgive one another in every situation and in every way. Whoever refuses to do this, may God grant him no rest and make his misfortune or plague ten times as bad. (*LW* 21:98)

Forgiveness is foremost in our Christian lives. It is a life-giving reality in two dimensions: forgiveness for our sin in Jesus Christ; and our forgiving and being forgiven by others.

Forgiveness of sins through Christ sets us in a right relationship with God (Rom. 5:1). But we also need peaceful relationships with others. We need to forgive sins against us and to ask forgiveness for our sins against others. Without this mutual forgiveness, the church cannot be all it should be, and we will be injured by unforgiven sin.

Luther said that as Christ "forgives us all sorts of faults, so we should bear and forgive one another in every situation and in every way." We remember Paul's words: "Be kind to one another, tenderhearted, forgiving one another, as God in Christ has forgiven you" (Eph. 4:32). Forgiveness is called for "in every situation and in every way," said Luther.

This is a hard word to hear and practice. To be honest, in his own life, Luther did not fully follow this. He did not always live up to his own theological insights. Luther needed forgiveness for not being forgiving. So do we. It can be satisfying to nurse wounds, lest slights and sores fester so that our relationships are poisoned. But forgiveness is needed. Forgive!

66. Continual Forgiveness

> By putting the petition this way and connecting the forgiveness of sin with our forgiving, He had the special purpose of making mutual love a Christian obligation, and the continual forgiveness of the neighbor the primary and foremost duty of Christians, second only to faith and the reception of forgiveness. (*LW* 21:149)

Luther pointed out that to the petition in the Lord's Prayer, "forgive us our debts, as we also have forgiven our debtors" (Matt. 6:12), Jesus added the provision: "For if you forgive others their trespasses, your heavenly Father will also forgive you; but if you do not forgive others, neither will your Father forgive your trespasses" (6:14–15). Luther said, "This is a remarkable addition, but a very precious one" (*LW* 21:148).

"By connecting the forgiveness of sin with our forgiving," Luther said, Jesus had "the special purpose of making mutual love a Christian obligation, and the continual forgiveness of the neighbor the primary and foremost duty of Christians, second only to faith and the reception of forgiveness."

This puts continual forgiveness at the forefront of Christian life. Mutual love is a primary obligation. Love for others—neighbors as well as enemies—obligates us to forgive, on a continual basis. This expresses love for others: we forgive them. No evasions. No excuses. Forgive.

Forgiveness is key in our lives. Forgiving others is "second only to faith and the reception of forgiveness" that we experience. The church is where forgiveness is proclaimed and practiced. As we pray "every moment" for forgiveness because we see our unworthiness, so we continually forgive—even as we have been and continue to be forgiven (*LW* 12:319).

67. Inward and Outward Forgiveness

The outward forgiveness that I show in my deeds is a sure sign that I have the forgiveness of sin in the sight of God. On the other hand, if I do not show this in my relations with my neighbor, I have a sure sign that I do not have the forgiveness of sin in the sight of God but am still stuck in my unbelief. You see, this is the twofold forgiveness: one inward in the heart, clinging only to the Word of God; and one outward, breaking forth and assuring us that we have the inward one. (*LW* 21:150)

Inward forgiveness in Jesus Christ expresses itself in the outward forgiveness we give to others. This is a mutual connection. My outward experience is "a sure sign," says Luther, "that I have the forgiveness of sin in the sight of God." Since I have been forgiven, I must forgive. My inward forgiveness makes me ready always to forgive others.

"On the other hand," says the reformer, "if I do not show this in my relations with my neighbor, I have a sure sign that I do not have the forgiveness of sin in the sight of God but am still stuck in my unbelief." Being unwilling to forgive surely shows I do not genuinely have God's forgiveness and am "still stuck in my unbelief." Liberating, life-giving forgiveness of sin is not mine if I do not forgive others.

This inward/outward circle must not be broken. What we experience inwardly, we express outwardly. For "this is the twofold forgiveness: one inward in the heart, clinging only to the Word of God; and one outward, breaking forth and assuring us that we have the inward one." How is it with us?

68. Forgiveness Does Not Depend on My Contrition

> Let it be known to all that I am not to make God's for-
> giveness depend on my confession and contrition. . . .
> This reduces the Keys and Absolution to nothing for I
> cannot be assured of the forgiveness of sins because I do
> not know if I have repented sufficiently. (*LW* 68:29–30)

Confessing our sins and a genuine sorrow for sin is part of forgiveness. We are contrite about sin, and we ask God's forgiveness in Jesus Christ. The promises of the gospel of Christ for
forgiveness, expressed in the Word of God and in the sacraments of baptism and the Lord's Supper, promise God's loving
forgiveness. We receive these promises by faith.

Luther was concerned that his opponents, especially the
Roman Catholic Church and Anabaptists, made "God's forgiveness depend on my confession and contrition." The danger
is that confession and sorrow can be turned into a "work" or
something one must "do" with a certain adequacy to receive
God's forgiveness in Christ.

Forgiveness is not tied to feeling penitent or contrite to a
certain level or degree. This would push people into complete
despair. For Luther, "We ought to place our hope in Christ's
word, not in our penitence." Forgiveness does not depend on
my contrition but on the promises of the gospel of Jesus Christ.

As Luther put it, persons are taught to "trust in the remission
of sins in proportion to their feeling of penitence. This means
they are taught never to trust in the remission of sins but to
strive for despair. According to the prophet we ought to place
our hope in Christ's word, not in our penitence" (*LW* 31:194).
We trust God's promises in Christ for the forgiveness we need.

69. Promise of Forgiveness
If We Have Faith

Here you have a sure promise, one that neither deludes nor deceives you, that, however many or great all your sins may be, in His sight they are to be as tiny as mere everyday human weaknesses, which He will not count or remember as long as you have faith in Christ. (*LW* 21:154)

Sin is serious for Christians. Yes, there is salvation by grace, and there is justification by faith. But we still need our sin forgiven. We confess in the Apostles' Creed: "I believe in the forgiveness of sins." So we do, through Jesus Christ.

God's promise to forgive our sins in Christ is firm and sure. This is our great comfort and hope. For Luther, "however many or great all your sins may be, in His sight they are to be as tiny as mere everyday human weaknesses." It is amazing! God can love us so fully and forgive us so freely that even our great sins can be considered as "human weaknesses." This may be hard to believe. We cannot "presume" on this—treat sin casually. Instead, we rejoice and are deeply grateful for God's forgiveness. Knowing it is completely undeserved, we realize God's grace is with us.

We receive the blessed forgiveness of sins in Christ, by faith. Faith enables us to believe that God "will not count or remember" our sins, "as long as you have faith in Christ." We receive forgiveness, "not because we have deserved it, but because He has won it all for us and bestowed it upon us." Faith in Christ is the gift God gives to bring forgiveness. Sometimes it is hard for us to forgive ourselves for our sins. So by faith, we look to Christ.

70. Christs to One Another

> As our heavenly Father has in Christ freely come to our aid, we also ought freely to help our neighbor through our body and its works, and each one should become as it were a Christ to the other that we may be Christs to one another and Christ may be the same in all, that is, that we may be truly Christians. (*LW* 31:367–68)

The forgiveness of sins in Jesus Christ is our blessing and joy. It is also a significant dimension of our Christian lives. We need to request forgiveness when we sin against others. We offer forgiveness to others who sin against us.

Jesus Christ has "freely come to our aid" and done for us what we could not do for ourselves: forgiving us and reconciling us with God and neighbors. Our Christian response is to love and serve others, "to help our neighbor through our body and its works." This includes forgiveness and making forgiveness tangible by rendering the help others need. When we think of Jesus, and particularly his cry from the cross, "Father, forgive them" (Luke 23:34), we realize we are most like Jesus Christ when we forgive and are forgiven, helping others, just as Christ has done for us.

Luther captured this when he said "each one should become as it were a Christ to the other that we may be Christs to one another." We "do to our neighbors as Christ does to us" (*LW* 31:368). This includes forgiveness, as well as all else Christ does for us and commands us to do for others.

This is a vision of the Christian life set before us and to be lived daily: Be Christs to one another!

71. Do Not Covet Honor

A preacher should not thirst for honor, the same as every Christian should behave. For no Christian, much less a preacher, has been baptized and called to eternal life in order to seek his honor. . . . Coveting honor is an extremely harmful vice, but nowhere so dangerous as when it gets in among preachers. (*LW* 68:101)

Our natural human tendency is to seek honor for ourselves. We like to be the center of attention or to bask in the spotlight of attention and praise from others.

Christians too are tempted by this tendency. We are not exempt. While we are not "turned in on ourselves" as sinners (see #8), we still sin. We still crave honor.

Luther cites this tendency to "thirst for honor" in preachers, particularly. But it afflicts every Christian. "Yet," said Luther, "no Christian, much less a preacher, has been baptized and called to eternal life in order to seek his honor." Seeking honor for ourselves is not what we were baptized to do! In blistering language, Luther continued: "There is no more potent or worse poison" than when we seek "honor in temporal things, honor that belongs to God alone." To take honor that belongs to God and to deflect it to ourselves "is an extremely harmful vice," and it is "quite dangerous if someone seeks nothing but honor."

These are appropriate words of warning for us in our media-driven world. When it is now easy for everyone to cast themselves in the most favorable lights and gain a measure of "celebrity" on social media, we need to heed Luther here.

Honor belongs to God. We are baptized to be servants of the crucified One, Jesus Christ. Beware of coveting honor!

72. Vainglory

There is nothing more harmful or poisonous than vainglory, as St. Augustine says, *Ambitio mater est omnium vitiorum*, that is, "Vainglory is the mother of all vices." It is the bride of the devil. (*LW* 68:102)

We don't use the word "vainglory" much anymore. It comes from the fourteenth century, literally meaning "worthless glory." It is inordinate pride in one's self or one's achievements. It is related to what we call "vanity."

Luther minces no words in denouncing vainglory as "an odious and accursed vice" (*LW* 27:115). He quoted Augustine who said, "Vainglory is the mother of all vices," Luther adding for good measure that it is "the bride of the devil."

This self-focus and overly high opinion of one's self is a form of self-idolatry, which puts one's self in the center of life instead of God. It is the opposite of God's divine grace because it assumes human abilities to do everything that is important, even if that is an empty form of boasting. This attitude can pervade one's life, affecting us fully. As Luther put it, "Vainglory is the most difficult vice to overcome, and is the true nerve and entire soul and life of pride and its heart" (*LW* 11:387). In another image, Luther said, "Vainglory is like a thistle: wherever you throw it, the prickles will always grab hold" (*LW* 68:104).

The opposite of vainglory is humility, focusing not on ourselves but on God. In all things we should seek to honor God and not ourselves. God's Word is our guide, not our own agendas.

73. Humility as Greatest Bond of Christian Love

This humility belongs to being a Christian as one of the primary and most necessary virtues, and it is also the greatest bond of Christian love and unity; as St. Paul says, again in the Epistle for today [Eph. 4:2]. (*LW* 51:351)

Humility, as Luther indicated, is "one of the primary and most necessary virtues." The attitude of humility regards "others as better than yourselves" (Phil. 2:3). Humility honors others in seeking their good instead of primarily our own. Humility is how we approach God, realizing God's greatness and our sinfulness.

Humility is not a characteristic we can honor in ourselves. As Luther put it, "True humility, therefore, never knows that it is humble, as I have said; for if it knew this, it would turn proud from contemplation of so fine a virtue" (*LW* 21:315). We can never say, "I am humble!"

Humility is the attitude formed when we see ourselves in relation to God and when we embrace others in love, bear with them, and serve them, as Jesus commanded. Humility opens us to others and their needs, making these become our concerns. So, for Luther, humility is "the greatest bond of Christian love and unity [Eph. 4:2]."

The clearest picture of this is Jesus himself. "For," said Luther, "we see in all the words and works of Christ nothing but pure humility" (*LW* 51:37). Jesus "emptied himself" and "humbled himself and became obedient to the point of death— even death on a cross" (Phil. 2:8). Jesus gave himself for us. In humility, we give ourselves for others.

74. Don't Notice Your Works of Mercy

> So our spirit and heart should always be overflowing
> in works of mercy, and not even see or notice them
> because of our great passion to be merciful and do good.
> (*LW* 76:291)

Luther constantly emphasized that "good works" do not bring
salvation. But those who receive the gift of salvation by God's
grace through faith will do good works. Works follow faith.

So, says Luther, "our spirit and heart should always be overflowing in works of mercy." This is what Christians do. It is
their desire to love God by serving neighbors. Christians seek to
meet the needs of others in every way possible. As Luther put it,
"love serves freely" (*LW* 35:72). Our service to others in Christ
are "good works" that we do—not in order to "do good works"
but to "love one another," as Christ commanded (John 15:12).

In one sense, the good works we do should be invisible—to
us. As Luther said of our works of mercy, we should "not even
see or notice them because of our great passion to be merciful
and do good." We are driven by the desire to spread mercy and
do good in the name of Jesus. Our good works occur, but we
move on to the next way of sharing mercy and doing good. We
do not keep track or keep score. We should not ever notice our
own good works. Like those in Jesus' parable of the Last Judgment who asked, "Lord, when was it that we saw you hungry
and gave you food, or thirsty and gave you something to drink?"
(Matt. 25:37). The righteous were surprised by what they themselves had done. They were astonished! So we should be, too!

75. In Despair
We Most Hope for Mercy

To the Holy Spirit it is not foolishness, but the high-est wisdom, that in a time of despair we should most hope for mercy while in a time of pride and security we should be most afraid. The prophet prefers this worship to sacrifices, and by his teaching he invites us, too, when we want to present God with a most pleasing sacrifice, not to sacrifice a hundred oxen or a burnt offering, but to sing this song: "The sacrifice to God is a troubled spirit," that is, to believe that our trouble and afflictions please God and to trust in His mercy. (*LW* 12:405)

Christian living means we do not see things as they "seem" but as they are from the perspective of faith in God. Luther often points out the paradoxical nature of faith. We live in the tension between outward appearances and inward realities.

On the psalmist's statement "The sacrifice acceptable to God is a broken spirit; a broken and contrite heart, O God, you will not despise" (Ps. 51:17), Luther says that it is in our times of despair that "we should most hope for mercy." While outwardly, in despair, it appears all hope is gone. But in faith, we recognize it is precisely in our despair that God's mercy is most active. What God wants of us—the acceptable sacrifice—is not out-ward works or actions, it is believing God will see us through our troubles when inwardly we give up everything to trust in God's mercy.

In the Holy Spirit, this is "not foolishness, but the highest wisdom." We should fear more when we are proud and secure, thinking we are self-sufficient. But God wants our whole selves to believe in and trust God's mercy.

76. Use Wealth
in a Christian Manner

The Psalm [62:10] . . . says, "If riches, money, and possessions increase, do not set your heart on them." For wealth is God's gift. You should not throw it away, but thank God for it and use it in a Christian manner. (*LW* 68:52)

We all have to come to terms with our wealth. "Wealth" can mean many things. Some have more than others. But we all have something, and our attitude toward our gifts is a matter of faith.

The psalmist said, "If riches increase, do not set your heart on them" (Ps. 62:10). This is the right perspective. Sometimes riches do increase for us. Luther advises to recognize that "wealth is God's gift." All we have comes from God. In everything we recognize that God's gracious benevolence provides our "wealth." As such, it can be God's good gift to us and "you should not throw it away," said Luther. God's gifts are to be used for God's purposes. This is why we should "thank God" for the wealth we have been given and "use it in a Christian manner."

The danger is that we will set our hearts on our wealth, seek it for its own sake—making money an end in itself. Then wealth becomes an idol. To rely on wealth violates the First Commandment because we are not trusting God. For Luther, "if God is within, the idol must go" (*LW* 68:54). We are not to be like the rich man who met Jesus (Matt. 19:16–26) for whom, said Luther, "the penny is his idol" (see #54).

Thank God for wealth given us, in whatever forms. Use your wealth for God's purposes.

77. Freed from the Fear of Death

> The Gospel does nothing else than liberate consciences from the fear of death so that we believe in the forgiveness of sins and hold fast the hope of eternal life through the Son of God delivered up for us. (*LW* 12:19)

Our theological thoughts are important and meaningful to us. But eventually, our thoughts meet up with our lives as we approach the end of life.

We all have a fear of death. We fear the unknown, and death is the great "unknown." From the beginning, humans have speculated on what happens after we die. Is there bliss or punishment? Or nothing? In ourselves alone, we do not know, so we have a natural fear.

The Christian gospel provides an answer for what happens after death: eternal life. This is the promise of the gospel in a nutshell: "For God so loved the world that he gave his only Son, so that everyone who believes in him may not perish but may have eternal life" (John 3:16). In Jesus Christ, our sin is forgiven. In Christ, we have eternal life—now and forever. Luther said, "The Gospel does nothing else than liberate consciences from the fear of death so that we believe in the forgiveness of sins and hold fast the hope of eternal life through the Son of God delivered up for us."

But when his thirteen-year-old daughter Magdalene died, Luther said it was strange to know that "she is surely at peace . . . yet to grieve so much" (*LW* 54:432). Luther's hope was real, yet death's reality was also devastating.

Our faith does not eliminate the grief death brings. But the Son of God was "delivered up for us." So we are freed from our ultimate fear of death!

78. The Worship of God

The worship of God means that you know, honor, and love God with your whole heart, put all your trust and confidence in Him, never doubt His goodness either in life or in death, either in sinning or in doing good, as the First Commandment teaches [cf. Exod. 20:3]. . . . This is the chief worship of God and the greatest thing, which we call a sincere Christian faith and love to God through Christ. Thus the First Commandment is fulfilled by us through Christ's blood, and God is very thoroughly served. (*LW* 76:122)

The worship of God is the most important thing we do. This is the corporate worship we offer in the church as the community of faith and our daily personal worship of God.

Luther reminds us that "the worship of God means that you know, honor, and love God with your whole heart, put all your trust and confidence in Him, never doubt His goodness either in life or in death, either in sinning or in doing good, as the First Commandment teaches [cf. Exod. 20:3]." Worship embraces our whole selves and all we do; it is our comprehensive activity, which reflects the deepest realities we desire: to know, honor, and love God. This we do with all that is within us. We entrust ourselves fully to God, in whom we place all confidence. Our faith is in God's goodness, which we experience in our lives and in death. When we sin and when we do good, God's goodness is faithful and constant.

We love God through Christ. This is our Christian faith. Through Christ's death, the First Commandment is fulfilled in us. Through Christ we can love, serve, and worship God.

79. Give God Praise

We cannot give God anything else, for it is already His, and we have everything from Him; we can give Him only praise, thanks, and honor. Psalm 116[:12–13, 16–17].
. . . Now "praise" is nothing else than confessing the benefit received from God and ascribing and referring this back not to ourselves, but to Him. And this praise and confession happens in two ways: first, before God alone; second, before men, and it is the proper work and fruit of faith. (*LW* 76:129–30)

If we ever think, "What can I give to God?" — we might come up with a pretty short list; or no list! Who are we to "give" God anything? What could ever be "adequate"? Of course, nothing we can "give God" can ever be "good enough."

Yet, as Luther says, since "we cannot give God anything," for everything is already God's; and "we have everything" from God — we can give God the only thing we can give: "only praise, thanks, and honor." All to God! This is what the psalmist urged: "I will lift up the cup of salvation and call on the name of the Lord. . . . I will offer to you a thanksgiving sacrifice and call on the name of the Lord" (Ps. 116:13, 17).

We praise God by "confessing the benefit received from God and ascribing and referring this back not to ourselves" but to God. We acknowledge God as the source of all benefits: "Praise God, from whom all blessings flow!"

We praise and confess our benefits before God. All prayer and praise is directed to the One who gives. We also praise before others, which is an expression of faith. Our great desire is to give God praise!

80. Do What Is Just

So how are we to serve our Lord God? Christ wants to teach this now and says, "Exercise justice and mercy, and believe," that is, "If you want to fear God with your whole heart, then abandon your idol and take before you the true God. Do what is just, and in doing so you will please God." He pushes that which was greatest to the back and brings forward justice. He is teaching the commandment in relation to one's neighbor so ardently that He forgets about His sacrifices. (*LW* 68:191–92)

One of Jesus' blistering critiques of the religious leaders was that they emphasized small matters while neglecting "the weightier matters of the law: justice and mercy and faith" (Matt. 23:23).

It is a constant temptation—and danger!—for us to do something similar. We can get hung up on the details and miss the big picture. We can "major on the minors" or get caught up with religious minutiae or trivia—certain matters of "proper practice"—so we miss the major emphases Christ wants to establish for his people.

Jesus targeted "justice and mercy and faith" as what is most important in relation to God's law. Luther zeroed in on justice: "Do what is just, and in doing so you will please God." Whatever idols we have—get rid of them; and "take before you the true God." Cast out the idols; and do what God truly wants you to do: justice. This pleases God. In this, we serve God.

Religious practices—sacrifices in Jesus' time—are no substitutes for right relationships with neighbors. Jesus, said Luther, "pushed that which was greatest to the back and brings forward justice." So should we!

81. Everyone Must Serve Every Other

A cobbler, a smith, a peasant—each has the work and office of his trade, and yet they are all alike consecrated priests and bishops. Further, everyone must benefit and serve every other by means of his own work or office so that in this way many kinds of work may be done for the bodily and spiritual welfare of the community, just as all the members of the body serve one another [I Cor. 12:14–26]. (*LW* 44:130)

Luther reacted against the church's traditional view of Christian vocation that God called men and women to serve in special ways, in a calling (vocation), to the religious life. These were as friars, monks, nuns, or priests.

The effects were to establish a strong clergy/laity distinction in the Roman Catholic Church but also to elevate those who had a vocation to be greater, better, more devout Christians.

Luther rejected the clericalism that gave clergy the most power in the church. But he also rediscovered the New Testament conviction that God calls all Christians and gives them the vocation to service. For Luther, "a cobbler, a smith, a peasant—each has the work and office of his trade, and yet they are all alike consecrated priests and bishops." All forms of work can be honored as consecrated—like priests and bishops. There are no differences among Christians.

Since everyone in the church is called, then "everyone must benefit and serve every other by means of his own work or office so that in this way many kinds of work may be done for the bodily and spiritual welfare of the community, just as all the members of the body serve one another [I Cor. 12:14–26]." Everyone must serve every other person as an expression of their calling. God calls all—to serve!

82. Do Everything in the Name of God

We have likewise been commanded to occupy ourselves diligently with the doctrine of the faith and of the divine Word and to begin whatever we do, whether early or late, in the name of the Father, Son, and Holy Spirit. (*LW* 68:150)

The people of Israel were commanded not to forget God's commandments. They were to write the Ten Commandments on their doorposts, on hands and foreheads, so the Commandments were always before them (Deut. 6:6–9; 11:18–20). Luther commented that "when they rose in the morning, ate or drank, they were always to remember God's Commandments."

Then Luther went on to say of Christians that "we have likewise been commanded to occupy ourselves diligently with the doctrine of the faith and of the divine Word and to begin whatever we do, whether early or late, in the name of the Father, Son, and Holy Spirit." This brings to mind Paul's admonition: "So, whether you eat or drink, or whatever you do, do everything for the glory of God" (1 Cor. 10:31).

Our total actions are to be expressions of faith and of God's divine Word. This is what propels all our actions. They emerge from our relationship with God and are oriented to obeying God's Word to us. This is a single-hearted devotion to doing all things for God's glory and in the name of the divine Trinity.

We need reminders of the fullness and diligence of what our commitment to "doing everything for the glory of God" means. In the midst of the busyness of life — including the doing of good things — it is easy to lose sight of our primary motivation. We need to go back to basics: do everything in the name of God!

83. Good Works for a Gracious and Loving God

There are so many additional good works that every moment of their lives they have an abundant number of tasks and opportunities to serve God. But these works, like the others, should also be done in faith, in fact, as an exercise of faith, so that nobody thinks he is pleasing to God on account of what he does, but rather by a confident trust in his favor he does such tasks for a gracious and loving God and to his honor and praise alone. And in so doing he serves and benefits his neighbor. (*LW* 44:97)

We are familiar with Luther's reminder that good works do not save us, but the Christian will do good works (see #26). The works emerge as an expression of faith for we are justified by faith in Jesus Christ. In Luther's words, "These works, like the others, should also be done in faith, in fact, as an exercise of faith." Faith is living and active. Faith propels us to loving and serving others through what we do. We do not imagine, as Luther indicates, that we are "pleasing to God" on account of our works. But we do what we do out of the depths of our love for God in Jesus Christ.

It is "for a gracious and loving God" and to God's "honor and praise alone" that we express our faith by our works. We have "a confident trust" in God's favor, and this is what we need to serve God freely by serving and benefiting our neighbors. There is no stronger incentive to active love than as an expression of faith in the God who is gracious and loving to us, a gracious love we see in Jesus Christ. Serve the gracious God!

84. The Church as Inn and Infirmary

> This life, then, is a life of being healed from sin, it is not a life of sinlessness, with the cure completed and perfect health attained. The church is the inn and the infirmary for those who are sick and in need of being made well. But heaven is the palace of the healthy and the righteous. (*LW* 25:262–63)

The Christian life is a life in progress. It is a progress from sin to righteousness, by the death of Jesus Christ. Our blessedness is in the forgiveness of sin and our "being healed from sin," says Luther.

Yet we are under no allusions that our life of faith is "a life of sinlessness, with the cure completed and perfect health attained." We continually need forgiveness—from God and from others. While we are righteous in Christ, we are still sinners—this is a basic theme for Luther.

But along our way in the journey of faith, God provides the church. The church is many things. But importantly, it is "the infirmary for those who are sick and in need of being made well." For the sin-sick soul, the church is an infirmary, a place for healing. For those facing all forms of "dis-ease" in life— whatever our problems—the church can be an inn, a place of refuge where help can take place. In the communion of saints, the community of faith, sisters and brothers in Christ can help us. Just as we, who are part of the body of Christ (1 Cor. 12:27), help and heal those who require our aid.

We need an inn and infirmary here and now. In the future, in heaven we will inhabit "the palace of the healthy and righteous." This is our hope and assurance!

85. Be Constant in Prayer

He especially says that we are to "be constant in prayer" [Rom. 12:12], that is, not stop or become lazy if what we ask for does not come quickly. The very best thing in prayer is faith which relies on God's promise that He will hear, just as He has said [Ps. 50:15]. If faith does not receive at once what it believes, then it waits; even if it appears that it will be diverted, yet it comes. (*LW* 76:226)

"Persevere in prayer," says Paul (Rom. 12:12). We are to maintain constancy and continuation in prayer. This means not to stop "or become lazy if what we ask for does not come quickly," says Luther. It is easy to become discouraged in prayer, to lose hope, or even throw in the towel. But we are to persevere— constantly—continuing to make our petitions to God, even in the face of long delays or the despair that may try to overtake us when we feel our prayers are not heard or answered. Today, Google gives us instant answers. Sometimes God's answers to prayer take longer.

But Luther advises, "The very best thing in prayer is faith which relies on God's promise that He will hear, just as He has said [Ps. 50:15]." The psalmist had heard God's promise: "Call on me in the day of trouble; I will deliver you, and you shall glorify me." The psalmist believed, and prayed.

Faith "waits," says Luther. When it "does not receive at once what it believes, then it waits; even if it appears that it will be diverted, yet it comes." In faith, believing God's promise keeps us keeping on in prayer!

86. Pray and Cry to God

We must above all else pray and cry to God in time of adversity and place our wants before Him. For God cannot resist helping him who cries to Him and implores Him. His divine goodness cannot hold aloof; it must help and lend an ear. All depends on our calling and crying to Him. We dare not keep silent. Turn your gaze upward, raise your folded hands aloft, and pray forthwith: "Come to my aid, God my Lord! etc.," and you will immediately find relief. (*LW* 19:71)

Jonah was in distress. He was "in the belly of the fish," having been swallowed on his journey to Nineveh (Jonah 2:1). Who could have had a greater need or "time of adversity" than this reluctant prophet?

So Jonah prayed, "out of the belly of Sheol" (2:2). This was all he could do. But it is just what Jonah needed to do.

Luther sees in this that "God cannot resist helping him who cries to Him and implores Him. His divine goodness cannot hold aloof; it must help and lend an ear." This word gives us hope. In whatever depths we face, we can pray and cry to God, believing God will help. Luther says God "cannot resist" helping those who cry to God. God's "divine goodness" must hear us and come to our aid.

"It all depends on our calling and crying" to God, says Luther. We pray and cry; "we dare not keep silent." If we do not pray, calamity will surely strike.

"Turn your gaze upward, raise your folded hands aloft, and pray forthwith: 'Come to my aid, God my Lord! etc.,' and you will immediately find relief," says Luther. Jonah prayed; and deliverance came. Help will also come for us!

87. God Will Say Yes

Never doubt that God in his mercy will surely hear you and say "yes" to your prayers. Never think that you are kneeling or standing alone, rather think that the whole of Christendom, all devout Christians, are standing there beside you and you are standing among them in a common, united petition which God cannot disdain. Do not leave your prayer without having said or thought, "Very well, God has heard my prayer; this I know as a certainty and a truth." That is what Amen means. (*LW* 43:198)

Doubt is the great enemy of prayer. We may feel that nagging, negative feeling—wondering if God will hear and answer our prayers.

But to this, Luther urges that we "never doubt that God in his mercy will surely hear you." For, Luther says, we are not praying alone. Though it seems we are completely alone, actually, we should "never think that you are kneeling or standing alone, rather think that the whole of Christendom, all devout Christians, are standing there beside you and you are standing among them in a common, united petition which God cannot disdain."

This gives us a new perspective, doesn't it? We do not pray without help. Indeed, "the whole of Christendom"—which means "all devout Christians"—is there beside us. All the saints of God are praying in solidarity with us. Together, a great chorus of petition ascends to God—the petition of our prayer! God cannot and will not "disdain" or refuse to answer this prayer.

This is great assurance for us. We are not alone. We can conclude our prayer with a resounding, "Amen!" This means, says Luther, that "God has heard my prayer; this I know as a certainty and a truth." Amen!

88. Christ Protects Us

For the devil hovers around in the air just like a hawk, but we are poor little chicks who stay under the wings of the mother hen, even as Psalm 91[:4] says. . . . Therefore, we must also do as the little chicks and crawl under the hen's wings. It is a glorious image that is rich and full of comfort, especially when we hold it up to the Lord Christ. For just as a hen leads her little chicks, nourishes and protects them until they have grown, so also Christ governs, comforts, and rescues us by means of His voice and Word, so that we are safe from the chicken hawk, the devil. (*LW* 68:248)

Psalm 91 is a great psalm of trust and assurance of God's protection. An endearing image is God as the protector who will "cover you with his pinions, and under his wings you will find refuge" (v. 4).

Luther describes the Christian as in danger from the devil, "in the air just like a hawk," while we are "poor little chicks who stay under the wings of the mother hen." This is a "glorious image," he says, "especially when we hold it up to the Lord Christ." Christ protects his own flock, as he said: "How often have I desired to gather your children together as a hen gathers her brood under her wings" (Matt. 23:37).

We are led and protected by Christ, "just as a hen leads her little chicks, nourishes and protects them." Through all the zigs and zags and dangers of life, we have courage. We are not afraid. We are safeguarded by Christ who "governs, comforts, and rescues us by means of His voice and Word."

89. Don't Forget God
When Things Run Smoothly

For who lives an hour without trials? I will make no mention of the trials of adversity which are countless. The most dangerous trial of all is when there is no trial, when everything is all right and running smoothly. That is when a man tends to forget God, to become too independent and put his time of prosperity to a wrong use. In fact, at this time he has ten times more need to call upon God's name than in adversity. As it is written in Psalm 91[:7], "A thousand fall at your side, ten thousand at your right side." (*LW* 44:47)

We all have trials throughout life. Sometimes these difficulties come so fast and furious that it seems there is something new—and disturbing—every hour. "Trials of adversity," said Luther, are "countless."

Yet, Luther points out that "the most dangerous trial of all is when there is no trial, when everything is all right and running smoothly." We may not recognize this. When things are going well we are in danger of forgetting God. We may "become too independent" and use our prosperity in wrong ways. This is such a danger that Luther says during these periods one has "ten times more need to call upon God's name than in adversity." In the "good times" our need for God is strong. We need to pray. We must recognize our dependence on God and our need to seek God's will and purposes; and we must know that all our blessings come from the Lord.

We may have "success" in life, however defined. But no matter how well things go for us, our focus must remain on God, trusting God and using the blessings we have been given to do God's will and serve others.

90. God Is Hidden among the Sufferings

The great thing in life is to have a sure confidence in God when, at least as far as we can see or understand, he shows himself in wrath, and to expect better at his hands than we now know. Here God is hidden, as the bride says in the Song of Songs [2:9], "Behold there he stands behind our wall, gazing in through the windows." That means he stands hidden among the sufferings which would separate us from him like a wall, indeed, like a wall of a fortress. And yet he looks upon me and does not forsake me. He stands there and is ready to help in grace, and through the window of dim faith he permits himself to be seen. (*LW* 44:28)

We need a basic confidence in life. We need confidence in God who, in the midst of what seems to us to be God's wrath or absence, is ready to help us in grace.

Luther cites the Song of Songs where the bride says: "There he stands behind our wall, gazing in at the windows, looking through the lattice." He interprets this to mean that while God is hidden as we experience suffering, God is still present. For God "stands hidden among the sufferings which would separate us from him like a wall, indeed like a wall of a fortress." When we feel an eclipse in the presence of God as we experience agonies, God is still there "gazing in at the windows, looking through the lattice." No wall ultimately separates us.

For God still "looks upon me and does not forsake me . . . ready to help in grace." "Through the window of dim faith," Luther says, God can be seen. This is the confidence we always need!

91. Entrusting Our Life to God

Think: "You see, not even for a moment do I have my life in my own hands. Now, since I have to entrust my body and life to God, why should I have any doubts and concerns about my belly and about how it is to be fed for a day or two?" It is like having a rich father who would be willing to give me a thousand guldens, and then not trusting him to give me a groschen when I need it. (*LW* 21:195)

Jesus said, "I tell you, do not worry about your life, what you will eat or what you will drink, or about your body, what you will wear. Is not life more than food, and the body more than clothing?" (Matt. 6:25). Our lives belong to God, and God cares for us. So we do not need to worry about the externals of life — food and clothing. God has us covered!

Luther put it bluntly: "You see, not even for a moment do I have my life in my own hands. Now, since I have to entrust my body and life to God, why should I have any doubts and concerns about my belly and about how it is to be fed for a day or two?" When we entrust our body and life to God, all else follows. God provides for our needs. We trust the benevolent care of our divine parent to provide for God's children.

Luther compared this to having a father willing to give us "a thousand guldens" — a tidy sum but then not trusting that parent to "give me a groschen" — a very tiny amount — "when I need it." We entrust ourselves to God, in matters great and small!

Present and Future

92. A Blessing Mouth

The Gospel is nothing other than a sweet, blessed, peaceful, healing word, which brings only blessing and grace to everyone in all the world; therefore, no curse may exist alongside it, but only blessing. For that reason, a Christian mouth must be a blessing mouth, not a cursing mouth. If it is a cursing mouth, then it is not a Christian mouth. (*LW* 76:228)

Christians believe and live the gospel. What is the gospel? Luther said, "The gospel is a preaching of the incarnate Son of God, given to us without any merit on our part for salvation and peace. It is a word of salvation, a word of grace, a word of comfort, a word of joy" (*LW* 31:231). This is the Christian message. The gospel is to be lived by disciples of Jesus Christ in word and deed.

The joyous message of the gospel should be on our lips. How can Christians be silent about the good news, which is "nothing other than a sweet, blessed, peaceful, healing word, which brings only blessing and grace to everyone in all the world"? This is the best news in the world!

So Christians should proclaim this message as blessing, not curse. "A Christian mouth must be a blessing mouth, not a cursing mouth," said Luther. "If it is a cursing mouth, then it is not a Christian mouth." We proclaim God's love made known in Jesus Christ, the word of salvation, grace, comfort, and joy. We follow Paul's instruction: "Bless and do not curse" (Rom. 12:14).

Is ours a "blessing mouth"? Do we have the gospel in our mouths, as children of blessing? Proclaim salvation and joy!

93. I Have Been Baptized

"[The devil says,] 'Behold, you are weak. How do you know, therefore, that God is gracious to you?' Then the Christian must come and say, 'I have been baptized, and by the sacrament I have been incorporated [in Christ]; moreover, I have the Word.'" (*LW* 54:86)

To Luther, the devil was very real. Satan was an accuser and tempter of believers, trying to get them to doubt and renounce their faith.

Luther asks what to do "when Satan speaks according to the law and says to you in your heart, 'God doesn't want to forgive you,' how will you as a sinner cheer yourself, especially if signs of wrath, like illness, etc., are added?" His answer — surely based on his own practice — was, "[The devil says,] 'Behold, you are weak. How do you know, therefore, that God is gracious to you?' Then the Christian must come and say, 'I have been baptized, and by the sacrament I have been incorporated [in Christ]; moreover, I have the Word.'" This is the Christian's answer! And the Christian's assurance.

In baptism we are incorporated into Jesus Christ by faith and are safe from Satan's assaults. Our lives are secure in Christ Jesus, no matter what any forces of evil try to do against us. The "the wiles of the devil" can be withstood! (Eph. 6:11).

"I have been baptized" is the response that vanquishes the devil! Satan's assaults are met by the greater power of Christ who claims believers as his own and clothes them in his protection. Our sin is forgiven, and in baptism, as Luther said, "I have God's promise of grace and mercy. I have enough. Whether night, day, tribulation, or joy befalls me, I shall nevertheless not forfeit His mercy or lose courage" (*LW* 5:59).

94. We Are Beggars

"We are beggars. That is true." (*LW* 54:476)

Among the last lines Luther wrote near the day he died was the short sentence, "We are beggars. That is true."

A beggar is totally dependent on others for the care needed to sustain life. Luther saw beggars on the streets in lowliness and poverty. They could make no pretense to honor or power. Their lives could be upheld only by the aid of another, who will give help.

Spiritually, Luther knew "we are beggars. That is true." Our lives as sinners, condemned by God's law, and in danger of judgment, give us no resources to help ourselves. We are alienated from God, unable to be reconciled or forgiven—unless our help comes from one beyond ourselves, from one source, alone—God.

And God has helped poor beggars! Out of grace for the undeserving. In Jesus Christ, sin is forgiven, and in baptism, new life is given. We are justified by faith, receiving the spiritual riches of God in Christ. As Paul said, "for our sake he made him to be sin who knew no sin, so that in him we might become the righteousness of God" (2 Cor. 5:21).

Luther said, "On earth we are beggars, as Christ Himself was; but before God we are bountifully blessed with all good things" (*LW* 24:84). Our blessings are in Jesus Christ. Now— beggars that we are—we are those who "as having nothing" are "yet possessing everything" (2 Cor. 6:10). In Christ we are "bountifully blessed with all good things," forever.

Christ came for us beggars. For "though he was rich," yet for our sakes, "he became poor, so that by his poverty" we "might become rich" (2 Cor. 8:9). Beggars, indeed!

95. In the Bosom of Christ

Just as a mother brings an infant into the bedchamber
and puts it into a cradle—not that it may die, but that it
may have a pleasant sleep and rest—so before the coming of Christ and much more after the coming of Christ
all the souls of believers have entered and are entering
the bosom of Christ. (*LW* 4:313)

There are many images for heaven. Some come from scriptural
passages. Others try to "imagine the unimaginable"—what
heaven in the presence of God and all the angels—can possibly
be like. Unimaginable!

Luther does not speculate about the glories of heaven or try
to describe them. He uses a simple image to describe the inde-
scribable wonder of eternal life. He speaks of believers, after
death, "entering the bosom of Christ." In a tender image of a
mother and an infant, Luther wrote, "Just as a mother brings an
infant into the bedchamber and puts it into a cradle—not that
it may die, but that it may have a pleasant sleep and rest—so
before the coming of Christ and much more after the coming of
Christ all the souls of believers have entered and are entering
the bosom of Christ."

This is the ultimate—and eternal—blessed life that awaits
those with faith in Jesus Christ. As Luther put it, "We must die
in faith in Christ, the Savior who has appeared; and after this
life we are gathered into the bosom of the Christ who was born,
suffered, was crucified, and rose again for us" (*LW* 4:312). Here
we "enjoy everlasting peace and safety"! (*LW* 4:314).

PERMISSIONS

These pages constitute a continuation of the copyright page. Grateful acknowledgment is made to the following for permission to quote from copyright material:

Excerpts from *Luther's Works* 1 © 1958, 1986 Concordia Publishing House. Used with permission. www.cph.org.

Excerpts from *Luther's Works* 2 © 1960, 1988 Concordia Publishing House. Used with permission. www.cph.org.

Excerpts from *Luther's Works* 4 © 1964, 1992 Concordia Publishing House. Used with permission. www.cph.org.

Excerpts from *Luther's Works* 5 © 1968, 1996 Concordia Publishing House. Used with permission. www.cph.org.

Excerpts from *Luther's Works* 11 © 1976 Concordia Publishing House. Used with permission. www.cph.org.

Excerpts from *Luther's Works* 12 © 1955, 1983 Concordia Publishing House. Used with permission. www.cph.org.

Excerpts from *Luther's Works* 13 © 1956, 1984 Concordia Publishing House. Used with permission. www.cph.org.

Excerpts from *Luther's Works* 14 © 1958, 1986 Concordia Publishing House. Used with permission. www.cph.org.

Excerpts from *Luther's Works* 19 © 1974, 2002 Concordia Publishing House. Used with permission. www.cph.org.

Excerpts from *Luther's Works* 20 © 1973, 2001 Concordia Publishing House. Used with permission. www.cph.org.

Excerpts from *Luther's Works* 21 © 1956, 1986 Concordia Publishing House. Used with permission. www.cph.org.

Excerpts from *Luther's Works* 22 © 1957, 1985 Concordia Publishing House. Used with permission. www.cph.org.

Excerpts from *Luther's Works* 24 © 1956, 1984 Concordia Publishing House. Used with permission. www.cph.org.

Excerpts from *Luther's Works* 25 © 1972 Concordia Publishing House. Used with permission. www.cph.org.

Excerpts from *Luther's Works* 26 © 1963, 1991 Concordia Publishing House. Used with permission. www.cph.org.

Excerpts from *Luther's Works* 27 © 1964, 1992 Concordia Publishing House. Used with permission. www.cph.org.

Excerpts from *Luther's Works* 28 © 1973, 2001 Concordia Publishing House. Used with permission. www.cph.org.

Excerpts from *Luther's Works* 30 © 1967, 1995 Concordia Publishing House. Used with permission. www.cph.org.

Excerpts from *Luther's Works* 31 © 1957, 1971 Fortress Press. Used with permission.

Excerpts from *Luther's Works* 35 © 1960 Fortress Press. Used with permission.

Excerpts from *Luther's Works* 36 © 1959 Fortress Press. Used with permission.

Excerpts from *Luther's Works* 68 © 2014 Concordia Publishing House. Used with permission. www.cph.org.

Excerpts from *Luther's Works* 76 © 2014 Concordia Publishing House. Used with permission. www.cph.org.

NOTES

1. Luther, "The Small Catechism" in *The Book of Concord: The Confessions of the Evangelical Martin Lutheran Church*, ed. Robert Kolb and Timothy J. Wengert (Minneapolis: Fortress Press, 2000), 354.

2. Luther, "The Large Catechism," "The First Commandment," in *The Book of Concord*, 386.

3. Erasmus, *On the Freedom of the Will*, in *Luther and Erasmus: Free Will and Salvation*, ed. E. Gordon Rupp and Philip S. Watson, Library of Christian Classics (Philadelphia: The Westminster Press, 1969), 47. See Luther's *The Bondage of the Will*, *LW* 33, esp. 103–17.

4. Luther, "The Large Catechism," "The Creed," article 3, #38, *Book of Concord: The Confessions of the Evangelical Martin Lutheran Church*, ed. Robert Kolb, Timothy Wengert (Minneapolis: Fortress Press, 2000), 436.

5. Luther, "The Large Catechism," "Baptism," *Book of Concord: The Confessions of the Evangelical Lutheran Church*, ed. Robert Kolb, Timothy Wengert, and James Schaffer, 2nd ed. (Minneapolis: Fortress Press, 2000), 465.

6. Ibid.

7. This is Mark D. Tranvik's translation of Luther's, *The Freedom of a Christian* (Minneapolis: Fortress Press, 2008), 50. Tranvik's is a recommended translation of this Luther work.

SELECTED RESOURCES
FOR FURTHER REFLECTION

Althaus, Paul. *The Theology of Martin Luther*. Trans. Robert C. Schultz. Philadelphia: Fortress Press, 1979.

Bainton, Roland H. *Here I Stand: A Life of Martin Luther*. Nashville, TN: Abingdon Press, 1950.

Ebeling, Gerhard. *Luther: An Introduction to His Thought*. Trans. R. A. Wilson. Philadelphia: Fortress Press, 1972.

Hendrix, Scott H. *Martin Luther: Visionary Reformer*. New Haven, CT: Yale University Press, 2015.

Janz, Denis R. *The Westminster Handbook to Martin Luther*. Louisville, KY: Westminster John Knox Press, 2010.

Kolb, Robert, Irene Dingel, and L'ubomír Batka, eds. *The Oxford Handbook of Martin Luther's Theology*. New York: Oxford University Press, 2014.

Lohse, Bernhard. *Martin Luther: An Introduction to His Life and Work*. Trans. Robert C. Schultz. Philadelphia: Fortress Press, 1986.

———. *Martin Luther's Theology: Its Historical and Systematic Development*. Ed. and trans. Roy A. Harrisville. Minneapolis: Fortress Press, 1999.

McKim, Donald K., ed. *The Cambridge Companion to Martin Luther*. New York: Cambridge University Press, 2003.

Paulson, Steven. *Luther for Armchair Theologians*. Illustrations by Ron Hill. Louisville, KY: Westminster John Knox Press, 2004.

Pettegree, Andrew. *Brand Luther: 1517, Printing, and the Making of the Reformation*. New York: Penguin Press, 2015.

Thompson, Deanna A. *Crossing the Divide: Luther, Feminism, and the Cross*. Minneapolis: Fortress Press, 2004.